Product Gems 2

109 *More* Science Experiments That
Demonstrate How to Build Products
People Love

David Greenwood

How Farmville turned the world into virtual farmers, why
Steam's Summer Sale keeps gamers indoors all summer,
how Netflix built a billion-dollar business on "binge-
watching", and over 100 more examples of the psychology
behind the most successful products ever created.

Product Gems distils research from 84 behavioural science
papers and case-studies into 108 bite-size "gems" that
demonstrate the key techniques used by leading
companies to build products people love.

For Mum. In the interest of fairness!

Contents

0.1. The Science Behind the Book

How each chapter has been carefully designed

Academic research papers offer fascinating insights into the way we think and behave. While they are full of incredible pieces of information, finding the relevant papers, understanding the terminology, and then figuring out how the findings can be put into action is very time-consuming.

This time investment required to digest research results in many companies overlooking the latest research entirely, with innovation suffering as a result. This book aims to solve this problem by distilling academic papers down into easy-to-read chapters to help decision makers quickly understand how the latest discoveries can help them develop, position, sell, and support their products.

I've divided the chapters down into clear sections (easy, intermediate, advanced, actionable) to help readers easily pick out content relevant to them. Each chapter gradually elaborates on the subject, or gem, to include more focused research. The chapters conclude with a series of Products Gems, actionable information from the research discussed.

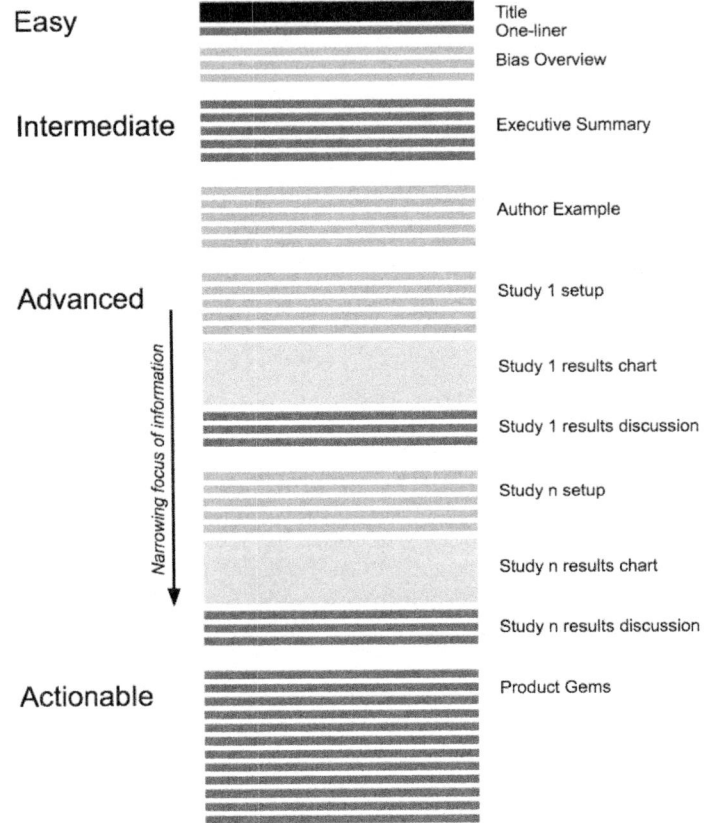

Easy — Title
One-liner
Bias Overview

Intermediate — Executive Summary

Author Example

Advanced — Study 1 setup

Study 1 results chart

Study 1 results discussion

Study n setup

Study n results chart

Study n results discussion

Actionable — Product Gems

Narrowing focus of information

Easy

Easy

You might be familiar with the acronym, tl;dr (too long, didn't read). Some readers will want to skim through information to help them hone in on what they're looking for or to perhaps quickly refresh their memory on a subject. The first few sentences of each chapter include the title (the subject), a one-line description of it, and an overview paragraph written to provide a brief introduction that can be grasped quickly.

Intermediate

Intermediate

Before jumping straight into the research, an executive summary is used to prime readers on the topic. Essentially, this is an elaboration on the overview. A "real-world" example of the subject is also demonstrated before more complex academic discussion is introduced.

Advanced

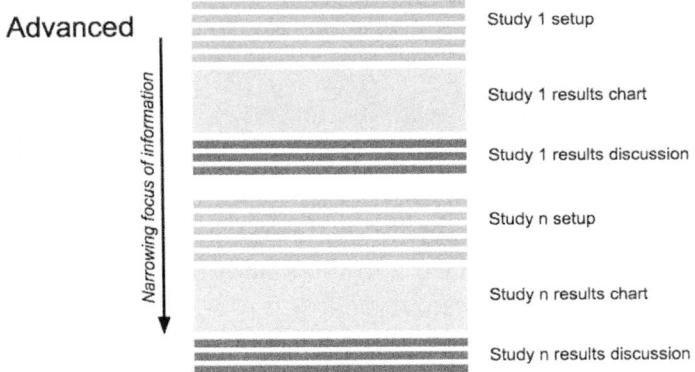

Advanced

Narrowing focus of information

Study 1 setup

Study 1 results chart

Study 1 results discussion

Study n setup

Study n results chart

Study n results discussion

The advanced section examines specific academic studies, describing the setup, the results, and what they mean. Graphs and charts are used to display the results from each study because research suggests that "illustrated text" is more easily understood that "non-illustrated text". It also allows the reader to quickly share the insights learned from an experiment more easily with others outside of this book.

Depending on the subject, a varying number of studies are introduced to the reader. The idea being that as the chapter progresses, the research will become more focused on specific areas of the subject and the nuances and limitations associated with it.

Actionable

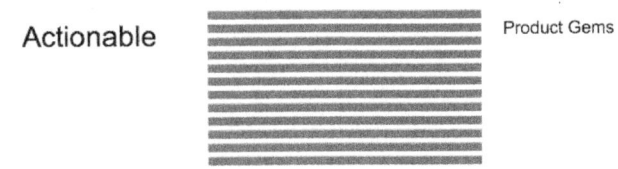

Actionable

Product Gems

The ultimate goal of each chapter is to provide readers with information they can take away and use. Each Product Gem is designed so it can be read before the content of the chapter and still be easily understood—and more importantly, be put into practice. If you read one part of each chapter, make sure it's the Product Gems.

0.2. Introduction

The Art of the Nudge

One late Spring morning during 2014 the auction room at Sotheby's New York was brimming with excitement. Inside were hundreds of people seated, with many more spilling out into the aisles. Those not in New York were listening intently into their phone or frantically refreshing the video stream on their computers to catch a glimpse of the action.

The auctioneer presided over this professional circus as the bidding for a 1-inch x 1.25-inch piece of paper steadily rose beyond one million dollars. Though the audience knew this was just the beginning. Sotheby's estimated the mint-condition item would make $10 - $20 million dollars.

As the bidding passed five million dollars a silence descended on the room. Momentarily it looked as if the bidding was over. Then, a voice called out from the back of the crowd. "Six million", the man cried, "Six one" another immediately called out. Any worry about the auction ending prematurely quickly disappeared as bidders continued to frantically outbid each other.

Each bidder was vying for a piece of British history from 1856; a British Guiana One-Cent Black on Magenta stamp that had already changed hands numerous times over its 160-year history.

Finally, an anonymous bidder on the phone submitted a bid of $9.5 million for the stamp, below the auction house estimate, but one that remained unchallenged by the other competitors. In just under ten minutes a humble postage stamp had managed to capture the attention of thousands, and that was just the start of it.

In the days following the auction, most major news media published the story of the "World's Most Valuable Stamp". Those outside the clique of collectors in the room reading the story over their morning coffee, baffled, questioned; "who would pay $9.5 million for a stamp?". Myself included.

As the adage goes, "one man's trash is another man's treasure".

In the modern world, this statement still holds true. Some will pay thousands for a car of their dreams whilst others will be satisfied with the cheapest reliable model. Others buy brand new designer clothes instead of the abundance of high-fashion items available second hand at charity shops. Said clothes can often sit in wardrobes alongside every colour of shirt imaginable, one for every day of the year, whilst others live out of suitcases.

Supermarkets shelves are stacked high with seemingly endless varieties of goods to entice hungry consumers. I'm one of them. Recently shopping for baked beans, I counted seven brands advertising the "tastiest beans". What was once a market dominated by Heinz, their slogan "Beanz Meanz Heinz" now seems outdated. Many retailers often carry numerous versions of their own-branded baked bean varieties from the very cheap to the very expensive, luxury options.

A survey carried out by British researches in 2017 found that in some cases these options had little, if any, differences in the ingredients used. Many were identical. Why is it then, that for exactly the same product some of us are willing to fork out a premium, quite literally, for the same product?

We all have different desires, different ambitions, and different preferences in life. Some of these are the result of evolution over millions of years. Mostly it's down to environmental factors though.

Every day we're bombarded with thousands of advertisements. You might be thinking that number is a little high. It's probably a little low. Advertisers target it us all continuously, and often subconsciously. Increasingly, advertisers are predicting what we're going to do next and then nudging us to their preferred outcome.

A nudge is a technique used by choice architects (as they're known in the business) to change someone's behaviour. Governments and policy makers are increasingly using nudges over legislation or direct enforcement. The UK's Behavioural Insights Team, more commonly known as the Nudge Unit, managed to boost the number of people saving for pensions from 2.7 million in 2012 to 7.7 million in 2016 by nudging the population (see: present bias).

Nudges can both enhance or dampen our inherent cognitive biases. In the book you're about to read I'll cover how our natural and nurtured biases lead us to make good and bad decisions and in-turn how product owners can use our shared cognitive biases to ethically improve the experience of consumers.

Someone once asked me if they could use behavioural science to build the next Apple or Facebook. The simple answer is; yes. Both these companies and many more have used behavioural science both knowingly and unknowingly to great effect. Though it is not that simple, as is life. Implementing all the *gems* in this book won't, on its own, lead to untold riches. But it will help you take a step in the right direction in building products people love.

Let's start afresh...

1. Fresh Start Effect

Goals set at a new, clearly defined period of time are more likely to be successfully achieved

We tend to motivate ourselves into good habits by using a new week, month, year or national holiday marker to put past behaviour behind us and focus on being better.

Every year on the 1st of January many of us will wake up to the guilt of overindulgence during the festive season. Some will aim to start the new year a little healthier; giving up alcohol forever, as the hangover kicks in. Others might promise themselves to give up bad habits, pay more into a retirement fund, cut credit card use, *or write a book.*

National holidays, birthdays, the changing of the seasons all provide a set marker in time for us to make a change. Similarly, job changes, moving to a new city, or buying a house are other markers people often use to set new goals.

More broadly, the notion that fresh starts are possible and offer individuals an opportunity to improve themselves has long been endorsed by our culture. For example, Christians can be "born again;" Catholic confessions and penance provide sinners with a fresh start; many religious groups engage in ritual purification or ablution ceremonies (e.g., Buddhists, Christians, Muslims, and Jews); and the metaphorical phoenix rising from the ashes is a ubiquitous symbol of rebirth.

Special occasions or temporal landmarks cause us to reflect on our lives in a big-picture way, which in turn inspires them to set goals for better behaviour. This phenomenon is referred to as the fresh start effect.

Highlighting meaningful occasions creates a clean slate for people to make better decisions. Temporal landmarks that signify a new time period -- a fresh start -- help us leave our missteps in the past and create an untarnished feeling for our present and future selves. This feeling opens the path for people to initiate goal-oriented aspirational behaviours.

Mint.com

As the tax year rolls around, many will be due a tax refund. When I first started working full-time, I'd hope of being one of these people. The overpaid funds could have gone a long way at the time, though often not on the most sensible purchases.

Mint.com is a personal finance-management service. Mint's primary service allows users to track bank, credit card, investment, and loan balances and transactions through a single user interface, as well as create budgets and set financial goals.

The service announces the arrival of a tax refund to users via email. The message takes advantage of this once-a-year occurrence to recommend an affiliate company, Wealthfront, who provide investment services that could be used to reinvest the refunded money.

The tax refund landmark, paired with the nudge to invest, matches the customer's goal to make smart financial decisions.

Gym Goers

Increasing the frequency of exercise is one of the most popular New Year's resolutions. In the following experiment, researchers examined the frequency of engagement in this important aspirational behaviour, exercise (Dai et al., 2013).

To do this, the researcher obtained a data set containing historical, daily gym attendance for members of a university fitness centre.

Researchers examined the attendance data against six calendar markers:

1. On the first day of the week (compared to the last)
2. On the first day of the month (compared to the 31st)
3. In the first month of the year (compared to the last)
4. In the first month of the semester (compared to the last)
5. On the first workday after a school break
6. In the first month following a non-21st birthday (compared to the last month preceding it)

Gym Goes (Dai et al., 2014)

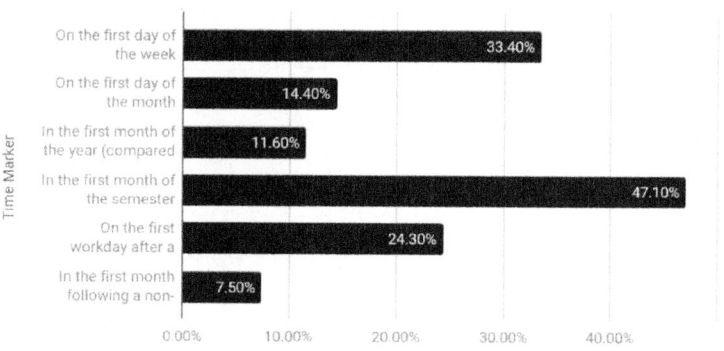

Change in fitted probability of going to the gym (%)

Members probability of visiting the gym increased at the beginning of a new week (by M = 33.4%), month (by M = 14.4%), year (by M = 11.6%), and semester (by M = 47.1%) as well as following school breaks (by M = 24.3%).

The research also demonstrates that personally relevant temporal landmarks -- namely, birthdays -- are, like calendar landmarks, associated with subsequent upticks in aspirational behaviour. In this case, the probability of visiting the gym is increased by 7.5% following birthdays.

Were more likely to conduct aspirational behaviours following a set new time period, assuming it has some personal significance.

Marathons (part 1)

Although humans age continuously, many societies divide the human lifespan into 10-year periods, or decades. In the English-speaking world, for example, people describe these periods as "the twenties," "the thirties," "the forties," and so on, which implies that human ageing progresses through discrete 10-year epochs.

Researchers believed that when approaching a new decade, or so-called 9-enders (29, 39, 49, etc.), people would be more likely to examine their lives for meaning (Alter & Hershfield, 2014).

They analysed participation rates in a domain where reporting a 9-ending age has distinct disadvantages: athletic events. Nine-enders are typically the oldest members of athletic age brackets, which divide runners into 5-year brackets (e.g., 35 to 39-year-olds). Researchers considered three age groups; 3-enders (23, 33, etc), 7-enders (27, 37, etc) and 9-enders (29, 39, etc).

Marathons (part 1) (Alter & Hershfield, 2014)

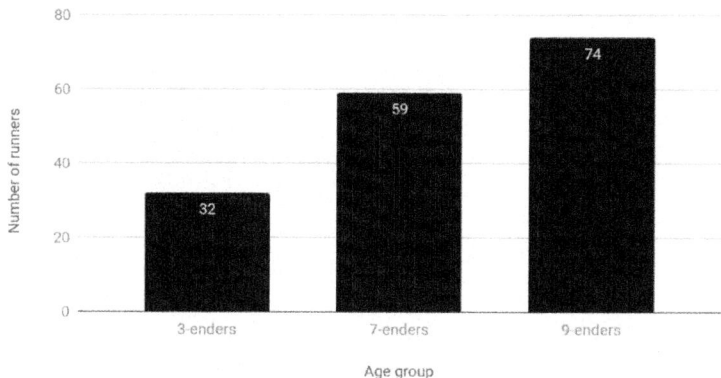

Out of 500 randomly selected runners, 74 were 9-enders, an overrepresentation of 48%. In contrast, there were 32 runners in the 3-enders age group and 59 runners in the 7-enders group, suggesting people got more aspirational as the new decade approached.

It appeared motivations to engage in aspirational behaviours were strongest in advance of age landmarks. Researchers believed this was because we tend to reflect on our lives and their meaning during such periods. New time periods can help with establishing new behaviours, by cleanly disconnecting the past and current self from one another.

Marathons (part 2)

Continuing their analysis, the researchers examined the final marathon times of the runners. They examined runners in five age groups; 0-enders, 1-enders, 7-enders, 8-enders, and 9-enders (Alter & Hershfield, 2014).

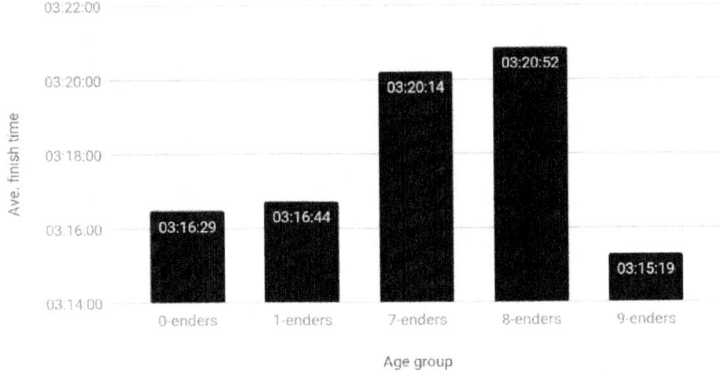

Marathons (part 2) (Alter & Hershfield, 2014)

Runners completed their marathons in an average of 3:15:19 when aged 29 or 39, their mean completion times were slower when they were aged 27 or 37 (M = 3:20:14), 28 or 38 (M = 3:20:52), 30 or 40 (M = 3:16:29), or 31 or 41 (M = 3:16:44).

Not only were 9-enders the most over-represented age group, when looking at the marathon timings they were also the fastest. Runners in the sample ran a mean of 2.30% faster at their 9-ending age than during the 2 years before and after that age.

Interestingly, 0-enders and 1-enders also performed significantly better, on average, when compared to 7-enders and 9-enders suggesting the fresh start feeling can inspire motivation over longer periods of time.

Fresh start feelings can persist for varying periods of time depending on the aspiration or goal set. The motivations that spur us to pursue new behaviours around temporal landmarks are tightly coupled to time (see: present bias).

Commitment Contracts

During our lives we commit to a broad set of goals that change and adapt as we age. A new job, a better house, or an improved work-life balance are current topics of conversation amongst my friends. From analysis already covered in this chapter, it would seem that the fresh start effect would help with any aspirational goal we set ourselves.

Testing this hypothesis, researchers obtained data from a website that helps customers achieve their personal goals by offering users an opportunity to specify consequences that will ensue if they fail to achieve those goals (Dai et al., 2013).

It is well-documented that goal-setting establishes reference points and is instrumental to goal achievement (see: goal gradient effect).

To create a "commitment contract," users first specify their goal and select a date by which they contractually agree to accomplish it. Next, users choose an amount of money to forego if they fail to achieve their goal. When users put a positive amount of money on the line, they also select a recipient of these stakes (e.g., a friend, a charity), should they fail to achieve their goal. Users can set a broad range of goals on the site, including those based on; career, diet, education, money and finance, and recreation.

Researchers compared the creation of "commitment contracts" around five calendar based, temporal landmarks:

1. On the first day of the week (compared to the last)

2. On the first day of the month (compared to the 31st)
3. In the first month of the year (compared to the last)
4. On the first workday after a federal holiday
5. In the first month following a birthday (compared to the last month preceding it)

Commitment Contracts (Dai et al., 2014)

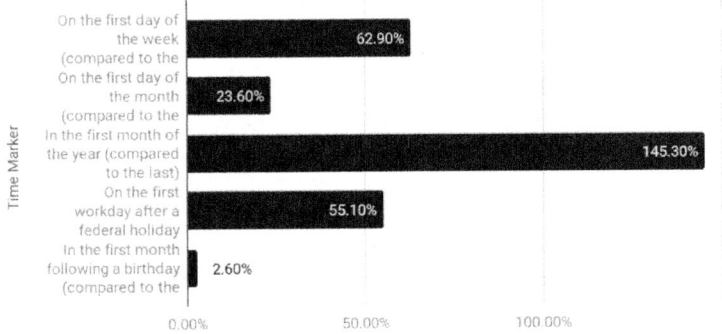

Change in probability of achieving goal (%)

The findings show that relative to baseline, people are more likely to commit to their goals at the beginning of a new week (by M = 62.9%), month (by M = 23.6%), or year (by M = 145.3%) and following federal holidays (by 55.1%) as well as following their birthdays (by M = 2.6%).

Further, the analysis provides evidence that the fresh start effect pertains to a broad set of health-irrelevant goals (e.g., career, education and knowledge, and personal relationships). This suggests that the increase in aspirational behaviours following temporal landmarks documented throughout this paper cannot be simply explained by the physiological need to offset overindulgence. Overeating, for example.

Temporal landmarks appeared to interrupt the attention to day-to-day minutiae, causing people to take a big-picture view of their lives and thus focus more on achieving their goals.

Invoices

"Cash is king", an expression sometimes used in analysing businesses or investment portfolios. It refers to the importance of cash flow in the overall fiscal health of a business. Healthy cash flow often relies on invoices for goods and services being paid on time.

In 2015, Vistr, a company that provides business with cash flow services, conducted a study examining the relationship between the date an invoice was issued and the time it took to be paid (Vistr, 2015).

The company analysed over 300,000 invoices issued monthly through their online platform.

Invoices (Vistr, 2015)

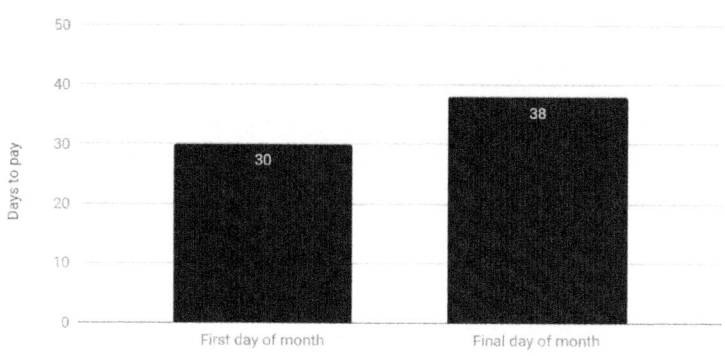

The average invoice issued on the 1st of the month was paid in 30 days. Invoices issued on the final day each month were, on average, paid in 38 days.

There are a number of factors that contribute to when businesses pay invoices. Though it is very likely the fresh start effect is a key factor. Invoices that are issued close to the start of the month can be accounted for in a timely manner as the month progresses with finance teams aiming to start the new month a fresh. Conversely, invoices that arrive later in the month cannot be realistically paid within the monthly cycle, before the fresh start begins, and therefore are rolled over to be paid in the following period.

We heavily weigh tasks, whether personal or in business, around temporal landmarks. Timing plays a crucial factor on both our own and our consumer's behaviour.

Product Gems

1. **Understand your customer's aspirational behaviours**
   How do they want to improve themselves? Do their aspirations change depending on the time of year? It can help to think of the larger goal first, followed by behaviours associated with achieving that goal. For example, a goal might be to get finances in order. An aspirational behaviour for that goal could be to commit to saving £X per month for retirement.

2. **Time messages to align with new beginnings**
   Consider pairing campaigns with special occasions, holidays, first-time experiences, birthdays, or other landmarks to motivate aspirational behaviour. The important thing here is to really know which occasions are most meaningful to your different audiences. Understanding your personas is key here. This technique can be of particular use to fitness centres and even luxury auto and retail brands that advertise an aspirational attribute to their products.

3. **Adjust content and messaging to make temporal landmarks salient**
   Highlighting a new beginning reminds people that time has passed; they can start fresh and work towards their goals. Remember, the goal is to highlight the separation of the past from the upcoming new beginning. Small labelling and copy changes are often enough to distinguish an occasion from other ordinary events. For example, framing March 20th as "The first day of spring" creates a stronger temporal landmark than "The third Thursday in March."

4. **Create a campaign across different time scales or periods**
   Framing certain days as opportunities for a fresh start can also be particularly useful to marketers. For example, a gym that advertises: "Have a healthy new year. Sign up for our new year's offer and get 20% off on your membership fee" may be reinforcing a desire to start a year with exercise. Fitness and diet brands tend to currently focus on large yearly campaigns in January, but they'd do well to focus on the power of a new week or customer birthday too.

5. **Recapture lost consumers**
   Identify and understand how long fresh start feelings generally persist in relation to your product and advertise accordingly. For example, the gym goers experiment showed motivation spikes on the first day after a federal holiday and declined rapidly afterwards. This implies the need to follow up with advertising messages that triggered the bias. Also combine fresh start feelings with other biases like the goal gradient effect, to encourage longer-term goal completion and reduce drop-off.

6. **Think about frequency**
   On the other hand, the study's authors suggest that in the case of behaviour that requires just one single action (such as donating to charity, getting a vaccine etc.), one fresh start advert may be sufficient to motivate behaviour change.

7. **Pull it all together for maximum impact**
   For single actions like this, perhaps when January comes, a donator could be reminded of their contribution the previous year, using that value as an anchor, and using a strategy that works upon

our desire to feel superior to our past self, as well as consistent with our decisions. For example, "You donated £10 a year ago, with your contribution resulting in x. Have an even bigger impact today by donating £15 for y".

2. Goal Gradient Effect

Our efforts increase as we get closer to achieving a goal

When people feel they have made some progress towards a goal, they will become more committed to continued effort towards achieving the goal.

At school, I noticed a typical pattern to homework assignments. Take a typical mathematics assignment. The questions were simple; almost too simple to start with, taking just minutes to complete. However, as the assignment progressed, the questions became more difficult and time-consuming. By the time I got to the extra-credit section, it seemed like the teacher had accidentally copied the work of leading mathematicians.

It was almost as if the easier questions warmed up the brain for the harder questions to follow. In turn, after starting the task, my commitment to the assignment deepened and it seemed harder to put the pen down until I'd reached the end. What seemed like an impossible task at the start didn't seem so difficult after I'd begun.

It's human nature to not want to leave something undone once we start it. It nags at our minds every time we're reminded of it and checking the last thing off or completing the final task makes us feel a little better. It's why so many of us have continued to play video games for longer than intended, reasoning that "we're very close to reaching the next level".

Tasks not started might remain that way for a long time, if not forever. Tasks that have been started are not only more likely to be completed, but as the goal moves closer, the speed of completion also increases. People are more motivated by how much is left to reach their goal rather than how far they have come.

Helping people to get started towards a goal will significantly increase the likelihood of them completing the desired task.

Steam Summer Sale

The Valve Corporation develop some of the world's most popular video games. Many of their titles build goals and achievements heavily into the gameplay, and perhaps surprisingly before you've even made a purchase.

Steam, the online platform where users can buy Valve's games, holds a yearly Summer Sale. For every $10 spent during the sale, customers receive one of ten Summer Getaway trading cards. Those who collect all ten, after spending $100, earn a Summer Getaway Badge that's visible to their online rivals.

During the sale, adding a game to your cart displays a progress bar showing how much more you need to spend to get your next card. Just showing that you've begun progress towards that goal is enough to create some mental tension over not having yet reached it, and some people are likely to toss in one more cheap game to get them over that hump. It's also clever of Steam to show you the progress before you check out so that you have one more reason to complete the transaction.

Of course, once you get one card, the effect happens again because you've now started checking off what you've collected from the ten-card set needed to craft the Summer Getaway Badge.

By adding a goal framed as a reward before a transaction is complete, customers are not only more likely to convert but also spend significantly more.

Microloans

The effect has been replicated numerous times, as I'll demonstrate. One of the more recent experiments examined the goal gradient effect in the internet age.

Researchers monitored 209 potential microloan recipients on Kiva, a crowdfunding site for microloans (Cryder et al., 2013). The Kiva website lists hundreds of potential recipients with information about their background, the nature of their loan request, and, most important for this study, the progress that recipients have made towards reaching their loan amount goal. Progress information is presented via both numerical percentages and a progress bar that is updated immediately when a contribution is made.

Researchers monitored the changing progress that loan recipients had made toward their goal at every hour during fundraising campaigns.

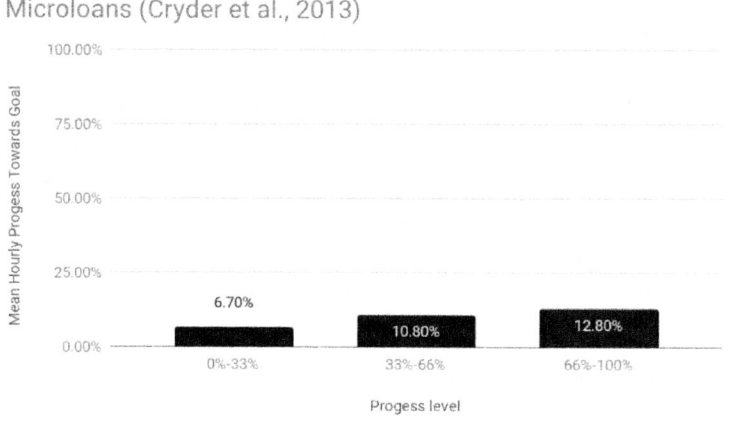

Microloans (Cryder et al., 2013)

During the first 33% of reaching the goal—that is up to 33% of the goal had been raised—fundraisers earned M = 6.7% towards their goal each hour. As funding progressed to between 33%-66% of the goal, M = 10.8% was raised per hour. In the final stretch of fundraising, people pledged M = 12.8% of the goal each hour!

The results support the hypothesis that real contributions increase as individuals approach their fundraising goals. Commitment to the campaign increased as the funding goal got closer.

Car Wash (part 1)

The goal gradient effect was observed well before the advent of video games and the internet. Many other experiments have found similar results.

In one experiment, 300 customers of a car wash were given loyalty cards (Nunes & Drèze, 2006). Half of the customers received a loyalty card that had eight slots to be stamped before a free car wash was awarded (zero of eight stamps, or 0% progress). The other half received a loyalty card that had ten slots to be stamped, but this time two of the stamps were already filled out, meaning customers only needed eight more purchases to get their free car wash (two of ten stamps, or 20% progress).

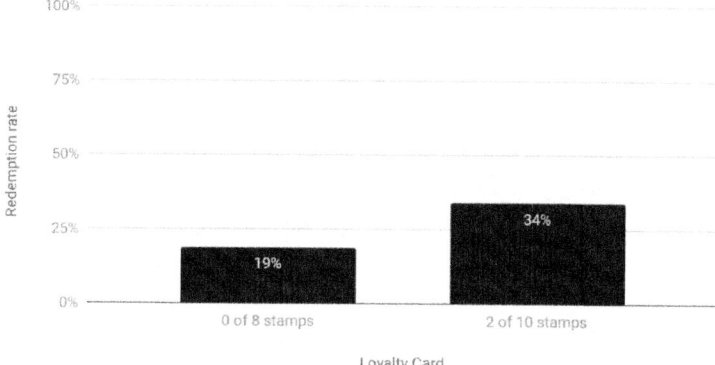

A total of eighty cards were redeemed providing records for 720 visits. The redemption rate for those given a pre-stamped card was significantly higher (M = 34%) compared to those who were given the blank cards (M = 19%). At first glance, the results don't seem very logical. Ultimately, both groups needed eight purchases before they could get a free car wash.

The researchers concluded that the head start loyalty card helped customers mentally reframe the completion process; the fact that they didn't have to start something from scratch played a meaningful role in their motivation to complete the card.

Car Wash (part 2)

The researchers then looked deeper at the eighty loyalty cards that had been redeemed by examining the number of days elapsed between car washes for loyalty card holders (Nunes & Drèze, 2006).

Car Wash (part 2) (Nunes & Drèze, 2006)

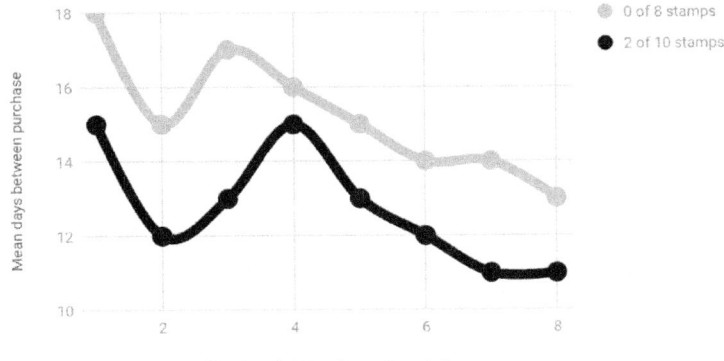

Mean days between purchase

○ 0 of 8 stamps
● 2 of 10 stamps

Number of slots redeemed on card

The results showed that those given the loyalty card with a two-slot head start returned, on average, 2.9 days sooner for their next car wash than those given the blank cards. **Those given pre-stamped loyalty cards were under the illusion they had already started their progress towards the goal and were more motivated to return for their next car wash.**

Furthermore, for both types of loyalty cards, the time between car wash visits decreased by 0.5 days on average with each additional car wash purchased. Those given the loyalty card with a two-slot head start took an average of 15 days to return after their first visit. By the 8th stamp, they returned in just 11 days.

As the car wash customers got closer to the reward, they increased their effort in pursuit of it, returning more frequently to have their cars cleaned.

Coffee Shop (part 1)

Loyalty or reward programs are very common; it's very likely you enrolled in at least one, perhaps at your favourite coffee shop. The next experiment mirrors that of the car wash experiment, though this time it considers a coffee shop loyalty program.

In the experiment, 949 participants, customers of a university coffee shop, were given a loyalty card that would earn them a free coffee after completing ten purchases (Kivetz et al., 2006).

Half of the customers received a loyalty card that had ten slots to be stamped before a free coffee was awarded (0 of 10 stamps, or 0% progress). The other half received a loyalty card that had twelve slots to be stamped, but this time two of the stamps were already filled out, meaning customers only needed ten more purchases to get their free coffee (two of twelve stamps, or 16.6% progress).

Coffee Shop (part 1) (Kivetz et al., 2006)

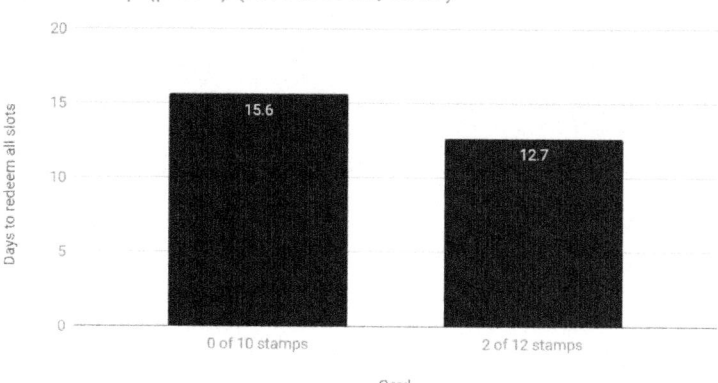

On average, customers who were given the blank card completed the ten required purchases in 15.6 days. Customer given the head start loyalty card completed the ten required purchases in only 12.7 days, nearly three days or 20% faster.

As seen in the car wash experiment, customers became more driven to reach the goal when they were under the illusion that they had already started their progress towards it.

Coffee Shop (part 2)

Many loyalty and reward programs are often designed with tiered structures. For example, airlines offer bronze, silver, and gold tiers with the associated benefits increasing as a customer earns a higher "status". Researchers hypothesised that customers might reset their increasing efforts to obtain the next reward (e.g., tier) once they had recently earned the last reward they were working toward.

Customers in part 1 of the experiment, who redeemed their loyalty cards for a free coffee, were then offered another loyalty card (Kivetz, Urminsky & Zheng, 2006). These customers were given the same type of loyalty card, either blank or with a two-stamp head start.

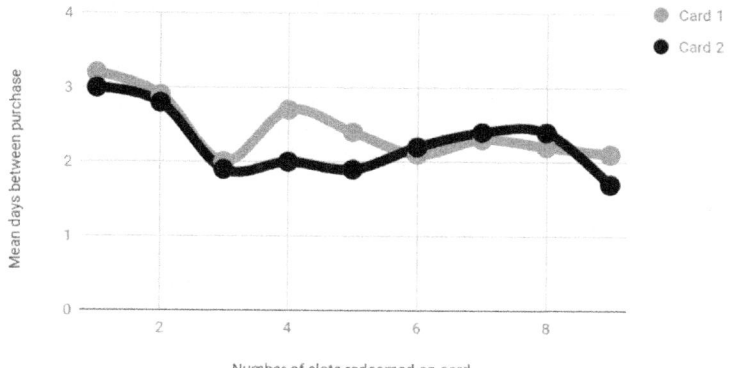

Coffee Shop (part 2) (Kivetz et al., 2006)

Researchers found the same goal gradient effect after customers received their first stamp on their first or second card; the time between their next purchase, on average, reduced over time.

However, when looking at the second card, they found there was little difference between the days to first purchase for card one (M = 3.2) and card two (M = 3.0).

There was a post-reward reset phenomenon; customers efforts were reset after reaching a goal, even with the next goal in sight.

Liquor Store (part 1)

We've observed how framing the path to a reward, by giving customers a head start, can increase their motivation. At times, such head starts can be viewed with scepticism by customers who believe them to be a marketing gimmick. For example, receiving a reward for no reason might seem odd to new customers, and even demotivating for loyal customers (see: lucky loyalty effect).

An experiment was set up using 240 customers of a liquor store (Nunes & Drèze, 2006). Participants were told that the store they were about to enter was considering launching a loyalty program. The participants were split into four groups.

1. The first group was told that under the terms of the program, after purchasing ten bottles of wine at a list price of $10 or more, they would be entitled to one bottle priced up to $20 for free (no head start).
2. In the second group, the required purchase amount was elevated to fifteen bottles, with one bottle being issued for each bottle purchased costing $10. The second group were also given a five-bottle head start to the loyalty program (No reason for the head start).
3. The third group were given the same scenario as group two, but this time were told, "Because you are here today, the store would credit your account with five purchases to start" (gimmick head start).
4. Finally, the fourth group received the same initial scenario as groups two and three, though this group of participants were told "As someone with your purchase record, the store would credit your account with five purchases to start" (realistic reason).

All participants were then asked to rate how likely they thought they would be to buy ten bottles in order to earn the reward on a 7-point scale from 1 (not at all likely) to 7 (extremely likely).

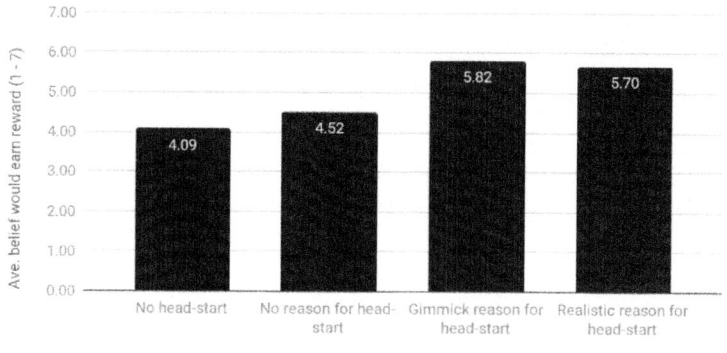

Liquor Store (part 1) (Nunes & Drèze, 2006)

The experiment was designed so that all groups only needed ten purchases of the same value to earn the reward. As expected, those not given the head start of five bottles at the start of the loyalty program recorded the lowest likelihood of earning the free bottle of wine reward (M = 4.09). Participants who were given a head start but no explanation as to why believed they were slightly more likely to earn the reward (M = 4.52).

Perhaps most interesting for marketing managers are the results for the gimmick reason group. An entirely arbitrary reason was shown to work just as well, if not better (M = 5.82) than a real reason based on a customer's purchase history (M = 5.70).

Creating the illusion of progress motivates customers towards a goal, and the way this illusion is framed has a direct impact on their level of motivation.

Liquor Store (part 2)

Researchers further hypothesised that the way progress was recorded towards a goal or reward might have a similar enhancing effect on the goal gradient effect.

The same customers used in part 1 were further divided into two groups (Nunes & Drèze, 2006).

Half of the participants were told that under the terms of the program, after purchasing ten or fifteen bottles of wine at a list price of $10 or more, they would be entitled to one bottle priced up to $20 free (measured in purchases). The other half were told they would earn 10 points for each bottle of wine they purchased at a list price of $10 or more, and after accumulating 100 or 150 points, they would be entitled to one bottle priced up to $20 free (points).

Like before, all participants were then asked how likely they thought they would be to buy ten bottles in order to earn the reward on a 7-point scale from 1 (not at all likely) to 7 (extremely likely).

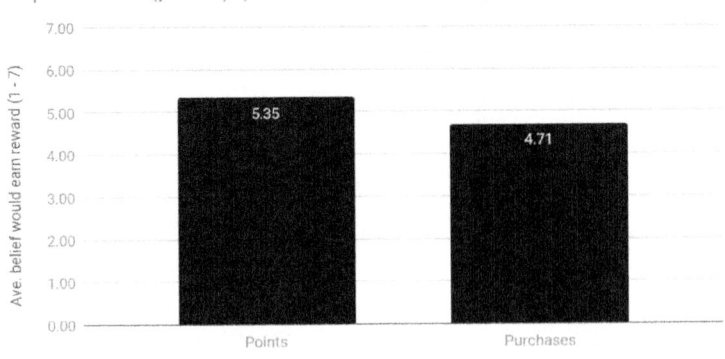

Liquor Store (part 2) (Nunes & Drèze, 2006)

Those working towards the free bottle of wine by counting purchases recorded a lower likelihood of earning the reward (M = 4.50) compared to those enrolled in the points-based loyalty program (M = 5.03), **suggesting that tallying one's progress in points rather than purchases intensifies the goal gradient effect.**

Product Gems

1. **Highlight progress**
   Making a customer aware of how far through a task they are can be a powerful motivator to complete it. Online retailers who show how many steps until the checkout process will be completed are a good example of this; "just one more step to complete your purchase".

2. **It's about gamification**
   As video games prove, gamification is more than just a buzzword. Making purchases about more than putting items into a cart, for example by introducing a challenge to attain a badge or giving customers the opportunity to earn rewards based on loyalty, can significantly boost the time, effort and money they are willing to invest.

3. **Give customers a head start**
   Helping customers to get started will significantly increase the likelihood of them completing a task or purchase. This could be a real (Kiva microloan progress) or artificial (pre-stamped coffee card) head start. The closer customers are to a goal, the harder they'll work to achieve it.

4. **Make goals clear**
   In line with your programme of incentivisation, heighten the sensations experienced as the consumer gets closer to the goal. Peggle, the highly popular casual game, uses sound in increasing tones to incentivise and encourage goal attainment.

5. **Break tasks into smaller parts**
   The shorter the distance to the goal, the more motivated people will be to reach it. This is why financial products can be very difficult to sell, as

their goals (returns) are projected far into the future. Break large tasks into smaller parts. For example, pension providers regularly send me material to the effect that I need to be saving a very large amount for retirement. Instead, they could tell me that by saving a certain amount each week, I could easily reach my retirement goal. Breaking the whole task into smaller, mini-goals makes it seem less onerous and one I am more likely to work towards.

6. **Remember post-purchase activity too**
   Think about giving new customers a head start during any onboarding. If they've downloaded your app, create the illusion of progress towards the initial setup. Users might give up on your app, sometimes in seconds, if the setup looks overly complex. If they think they've already started the task, they will be less likely to give up.

7. **Increase brand and product interactions**
   As seen in the car wash experiment, people visited more frequently as they got closer to a free car wash. The goal gradient effect can be a powerful revenue booster for businesses that rely on regular customer interaction.

8. **Use to boost loyalty programs**
   The goal gradient effect can be used as a powerful marketing tool for loyalty programs. Incentivise initial adoption using the illusion of progress, but remember it is important how you frame any progress towards a goal. While the reason for the head start can be arbitrary, tallying a customer's progress in points rather than purchases will intensify the goal gradient effect.

9. **Crowdfunders take note**
   As researchers discovered when studying Kiva,

donations and donors increased the closer a campaign was to meeting its goal. While you can't artificially inflate progress during crowdfunding campaigns, making sure you have early backers to pledge towards your goal will motivate others stumbling across your campaign to do the same.

10. **Beware of post-reward reset**

Customers' motivation has a tendency to initially drop to the baseline after a goal has been reached. This is the case even if there is a second reward on the horizon. This is the point at which you are most likely to lose your customer. Think of ways to counterbalance this, potentially through staff training, targeted marketing or random rewards that sit outside of the perceived loyalty structure.

3. Motivating-Uncertainty Effect

We're more motivated to reach a goal with an uncertain reward

Uncertainty is more powerful than certainty in boosting motivation towards a goal, making us work harder, spend more and enjoy more in the process. Uncertainty about positive outcomes stimulates positive feelings and arousal.

After reading this chapter, you've got an equal chance of coming away with either:

1. A sense of enlightenment about how the effect works; or
2. Information you can use to significantly improve the adoption and utilisation of your products.

Whichever of the two you take away from reading this chapter, what's clear is that the uncertainty of not knowing what reward you'll get will help compel you to reach the goal of completing the chapter.

This might sound odd at first. As emotional humans, we're typically risk-averse, often preferring certainty over uncertainty (Bernoulli, 1738; von Neumann & Morgenstern, 1944; Kahneman & Tversky, 1979). Despite our craving for certainty, uncertainty can be used as a powerful motivator.

The motivating-uncertainty effect can be used to get customers to invest effort, time, and money, both in pursuit of your products and desired behaviours.

Premium Bonds

The UK government offers a financial savings product called premium bonds. Each month, a prize draw is conducted for bondholders with prizes ranging from £25 up to £1 million. Each £1 bond held by an investor buys one entry into the monthly draw, and each bond has an equal chance of winning. The more premium bonds an investor holds, the greater their chances of winning a prize improves.

More than 22 million UK citizens, about one-third of the population, have invested over £68 billion in premium bonds despite the interest rate they offer is well below that offered by other savings products. The reality is, unless you win one of the very large prizes, you will be worse off holding premium bonds than investing elsewhere.

So why are they so popular? It's down to uncertainty. Uncertainty creates more positive, exciting experiences. We get excited by the unknown. **Uncertainty increases one's investment of effort, time, and money in pursuing rewards—even when the outcome is likely to be worse than more certain alternatives.**

Drink of Water

One experiment that studied whether uncertain rewards increase motivation involved eighty-seven college students from the University of Chicago who were challenged to drink 1.4 litres (47 Oz.) of water in under two minutes (Shen et al., 2015).

The participants were split into two groups. One group was told they'd receive $2 for completing the challenge successfully. Those in the other group was told they'd receive either $1 or $2, with the outcome dictated by a coin toss following the successful completion of the task.

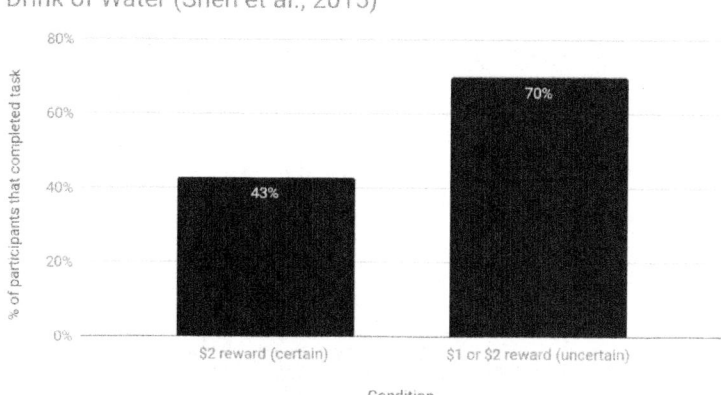

Drink of Water (Shen et al., 2015)

In the experiment, 70% of participants in the group faced with the uncertain reward completed the task, compared to 43% in the group with the guaranteed reward of $2. A surprising result considering, at best, the uncertain group would receive a reward equal to the certain group, but also potentially a clearly inferior reward!

This first experiment demonstrates that uncertainty increases motivation to complete a task.

Marketing Survey

The researchers pondered if motivation correlated to the probability of receiving a reward. To test this hypothesis, they asked 530 participants to complete a marketing survey that required them to rate a number of print advertisements on a scale of 1 (very bad) to 10 (very good) (Shen et al., 2015).

In return for rating sixty advertisements, each participant was told they would receive a payment of $1.

Participants were also told they would receive a bonus of either $0.20 or $0.50 for completing extra work by rating more advertisements. The participants were split into eight groups with each group given different probabilities of their eligibility to receive the higher $0.50 bonus (0%, 1%, 40%, 50%, 60%, 99%, 100%, and unspecified).

Marketing survey (Shen et al., 2015)

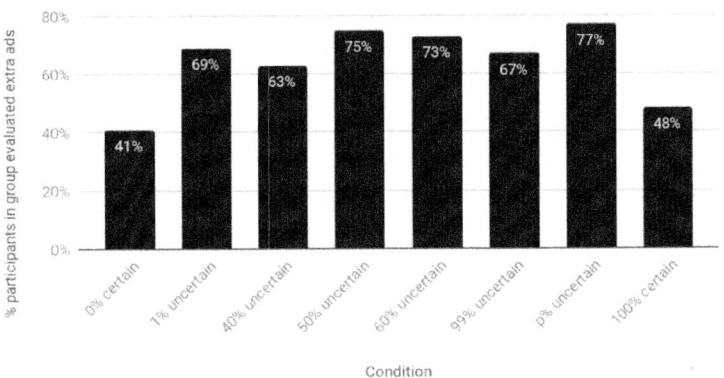

Of the eight groups, six were faced with uncertain rewards. The percentage of participants in these six groups that completed the extra work was significantly higher than in the two certain reward groups, 0% certain ($0.20 bonus) when 41% completed the extra work and 100% certain ($0.50) when 48% completed it. When the higher reward was completely unknown (% uncertain), the largest number of students, 77%, completed the extra work.

Regardless of whether the reward probability is specified, and regardless of what the specified probability is, adding uncertainty to rewards significantly boosts motivation towards a goal.

Truffle Auction

In another experiment, researchers asked 138 students to bid on a bag of Godiva chocolate truffles (Shen et al., 2015). Half of the participants were shown a bag containing four truffles. The other half weren't shown the contents, but they were told by a researcher posing as an auctioneer that there was an equal chance of the bag containing either two or four truffles.

Participants were then told an auction would be conducted allowing them to bid on the truffles. However, before bidding started, half of both groups were also asked an extra question in advance:

"What's the highest you'd bid for the chocolates?"

This was done to compare how keen both groups would be to pay for certainty before starting the exciting bidding process.

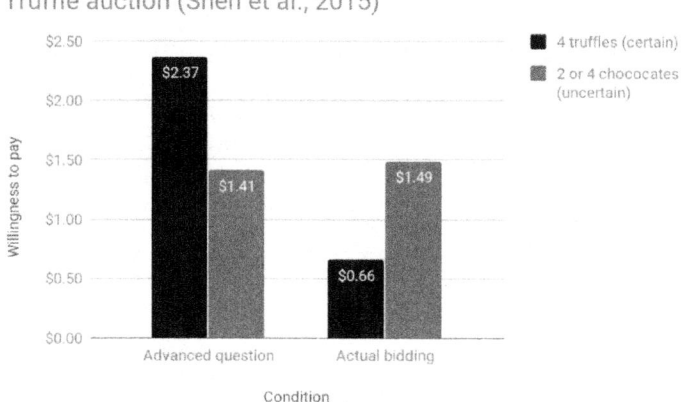

Truffle auction (Shen et al., 2015)

Those who were offered the certain bag of four truffles and asked in advance how much they'd be willing to pay offered $1.71 more than the winning bid offered by the other half of their group who took part in the auction (M = $2.37 vs M = $0.66).

Clearly, we prefer certainty when asked up front. We're inherently risk-averse (Gneezy & List, 2006; Kahneman & Tversky 1979), but only when our focus is on the outcome.

It gets really interesting when looking at the results of those told the bag they would be bidding on contained either two or four truffles. The bidding group for the uncertain bag ended up being willing to pay 125% more than those certain they were bidding on the four-truffle bag (M = $1.49 vs M = $0.66).

In this case, the participants paid much more for the uncertain reward. It seems the shift in focus towards the auction process, rather than the outcome, caused this shift in behaviour (see: present bias).

Chocolate Coins (part 1)

This left the researchers scratching their heads, as you might also be doing. A final experiment was conducted to test why people were willing to pay more for an uncertain reward in certain situations, for example, at auction.

In this experiment, 158 Chicago residents were asked to bid on cups of chocolate coins (Shen et al., 2015). The participants were split in half. One-half of the participants were shown a cup containing five coins. The second half were told the cup had an equal chance of containing either three, four or five coins.

Just before the bidding started, half of the participants from each group were told either:

1. "Enjoy the auction" (focus on the process)
2. "The auctions are a way to get the coins at a good price" (focus on the outcome)

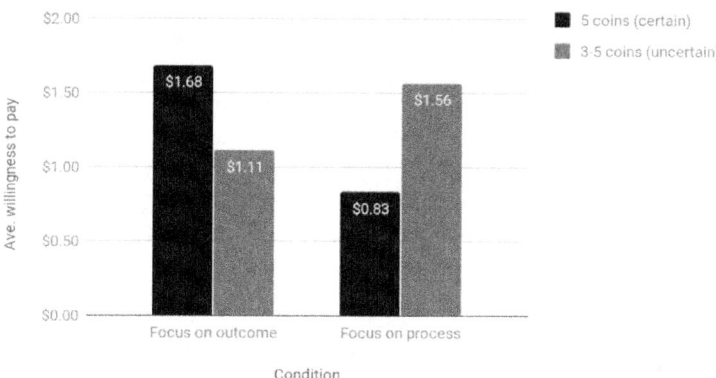

Those focusing on the outcome were willing to pay more (M = $1.68) than those focusing on the process (M = $0.83) for the certain reward. This was not true of those who were bidding on the uncertain reward, who were willing to pay more when focusing on the process (M = $1.56), the auction itself, than when focusing on the outcome, getting the coins (M = $1.11).

Those who were bidding on the uncertain reward were willing to pay almost twice as much (M = $1.56) as those bidding on the certain reward when focusing on the process ($0.83), even though the outcome was 66% likely to be worse for the uncertain bidders.

Drawing people's attention to the process (vs outcome) of gaining a reward makes them willing to

pay more for uncertainty, even when the outcome is likely to be worse.

Chocolate Coins (part 2)

As part of the same experiment, the researchers also asked the participants a series of questions designed to rate their experience of the auction process (Shen et al., 2015). From the participant's answers, a "process experience index" was created, essentially ranking a participant's experience from 0 (bad) to 9 (good).

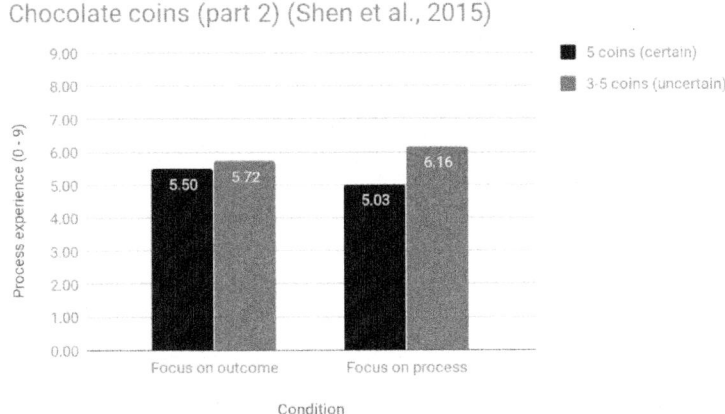

Chocolate coins (part 2) (Shen et al., 2015)

Not only were participants willing to pay more when focusing on the process, those who were bidding on the uncertain reward also reported feeling far more interest and excitement during the auction process (M = 5.72 and M = 6.16 for outcome and process conditions respectively) than those bidding on the certain reward (M = 5.50 and M = 5.03 for outcome and process conditions respectively).

Drawing people's attention to the process (vs outcome) of reward pursuits makes them evaluate the experience more positively.

Product Gems

1. **Uncertain rewards can increase investment**
   We're more likely to invest more effort, time, and money in pursuing rewards of an uncertain nature.

2. **Uncertain rewards are less expensive to put in place**
   We're more motivated to get an uncertain reward that has a lower potential value, as backward as that seems. Take the truffle example, where people were willing to pay for the risk of receiving less.

3. **Uncertainty can increase enjoyment**
   It can be used to create a more fun and exciting process on route to a given goal. It's useful for fostering motivation in workplace systems that are compulsory. Or, it could be used for tasks that are a little boring and in need of some uncertainty-generated excitement.

4. **Boost team productivity**
   Consider offering uncertain rewards to your best-performing employees. For example, the first salesperson to sell a certain amount qualifies for the opportunity to win a prize of value between $1000–$2000. However, make sure they focus on the process of achieving the reward. Perhaps display each deal they make on a reward leaderboard table.

5. **Change consumer behaviour**
   We're more motivated to achieve goals when the reward is uncertain. For consumer health-based products, this could be especially powerful. Keeping to a calorie goal for a given period within a health-tracking app, for example. Focusing on the journey rather than the destination seems to be a

better way of staying on track and motivated because the feeling is the goal.

6. **Use in loyalty programmes**
   Consider adding an uncertain reward to existing loyalty programmes. Attract people with a certain reward, then foster ongoing motivation and higher return rates with use of uncertain rewards and emphasis on the process.

7. **Keep in mind reward size**
   As the size of the reward gets increases, the effect will most likely lessen, as we shift greater attention to the outcome than to the process of attaining it.

8. **Opportunity for new business models**
   There is clear potential for new types of auction systems that focus more on the exciting process of bidding over an uncertain reward.

9. **May have a stronger effect on certain personality types**
   The effect might work best with 'sensation-seekers'; those who have a craving for and desire to seek out positive experiences (Zuckerman, 2007).

4. Zeigarnik Effect

Uncompleted tasks stick in our minds more than completed ones

Whether it's a waiter recalling a long order, a meaningful consumer transaction or a cliff-hanger on Netflix, tasks heavily occupy our minds until complete.

Growing up in the UK, I remember watching a television programme shown on Saturday nights called The Generation Game. At the end of the show, one member of the victorious team watched twenty prizes pass on a conveyor belt and then won as many as they could recall in forty-five seconds afterwards.

Many contestants, and those playing in front of their TV (me), regularly recalled fifteen or more of the items. Recalling all twenty items might seem very challenging. Although unlike many games that are designed to minimise players winnings, the final of The Generation Game gave the players a cognitive advantage.

It turns out that a task that has already been started establishes a task-specific tension, which improves cognitive access to any relevant information. The tension that has been established is relieved upon successful completion of the task. If the task is interrupted, any reduction of tension is impeded. With continuous tension, the relevant information becomes more accessible and more easily remembered.

This phenomenon is known as the Zeigarnik effect, named after Soviet psychologist and psychiatrist Bluma Zeigarnik (1901–1988) who was one of the first people to conduct research into the effect.

If you look around you, you will start to notice the Zeigarnik effect everywhere. It is especially used in media and advertising. Have you ever wondered why cliff-hangers work so well or why you just can't get yourself to stop watching a series on Netflix? Just one more chapter...

Waiting Staff

It's summer 2007. I had just left sixth-form college (high school) and was working a part-time job waiting tables, saving money with dreams of travelling the world.

> *Table 1: 1x Margherita Pizza (extra cheese), 1x Risotto Pollo e Asparagi, 1x bottle of red wine*
> *Table 2: 1x Spaghetti Carbonara, 1x Fusilli Al Forno, 1x bottle of white wine*
> *Table 3: 1x Filetto Rossini, 1x Spigola alla Genovese, 2x bottles of beer*

These orders are all made up. I can barely recall the menu today. Research and experience would suggest I would have remembered these orders up until the point of handing them over to the hungry customers.

Similarly, while studying at the University of Berlin a student, Bluma Zeigarnik, and her professor, Kurt Lewin, had noted how waiters in a cafe seemed to remember incomplete tabs more efficiently than those that had been paid for and were complete.

Lewin suggested that the mere completion of a task can lead to it being forgotten, while incomplete tasks, such as serving guests at a table who have not yet eaten, are better remembered.

Puzzles (part 1)

In this experiment, 164 participants were told they would be given a series of eighteen to twenty-two tasks to complete (Zeigarnik, 1927). Each participant was given the tasks one at a time, and they ranged from manual work (constructing a box of cardboard, making clay figures, etc.) to mental problems such as puzzles or maths questions.

The participants were allowed to finish half of the tasks, but were interrupted during the other half. The order and type of interruption was such that no one could suspect the reason. Following the experiment, the participants were asked to recall the tasks they had worked on:

> *"Please tell me what the tasks were upon which you worked during this experiment."*

Puzzles (part 1) (Zeigarnik, 1927)

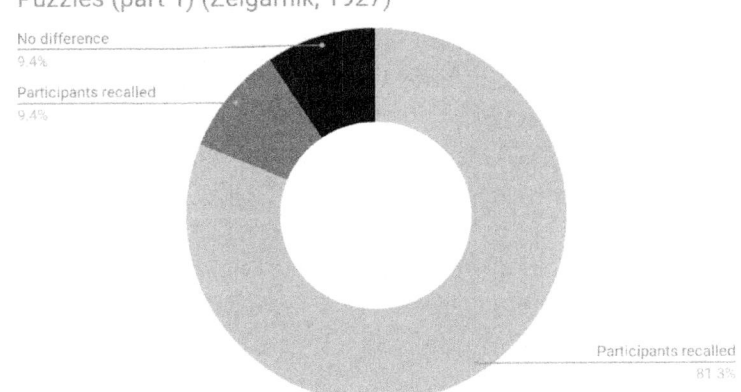

No difference
9.4%

Participants recalled
9.4%

Participants recalled
81.3%

The results revealed that 81.3% of participants remembered interrupted tasks best, 9.4% remembered the completed and interrupted ones equally well, and 9.4% remembered the completed better than the interrupted. The results showed that interrupted tasks were remembered nine times better than completed tasks!

When recalling the order of the tasks, participants also mentioned the interrupted tasks first three times as often as the completed ones.

The study suggests that uncompleted tasks can often remain as intentions and, as such, they remain in memory. We are better at remembering the details of incomplete tasks.

Puzzles (part 2)

Zeigarnik pondered if age had an impact on the effect. To test this, an experiment was conducted with two groups of forty-seven adults and forty-five school children (average age of the latter, fourteen years) (Zeigarnik, 1927).

In this experiment, the participants were given eighteen tasks to complete. The material for each was presented in a separate envelope. The tasks were similar to those in part 1 of the experiment. At the word "begin" each subject opened the first envelope, read the instructions for that task and began work. As soon as they had finished, or immediately upon being told to stop, the entire contents of the task were returned to the envelope.

All participants began each new task at the same time. As some worked faster than others, the instructions to stop were given when approximately half of the group had completed a given task, the other half of participants were therefore interrupted before completion.

Puzzles (part 2) (Zeigarnik, 1927)

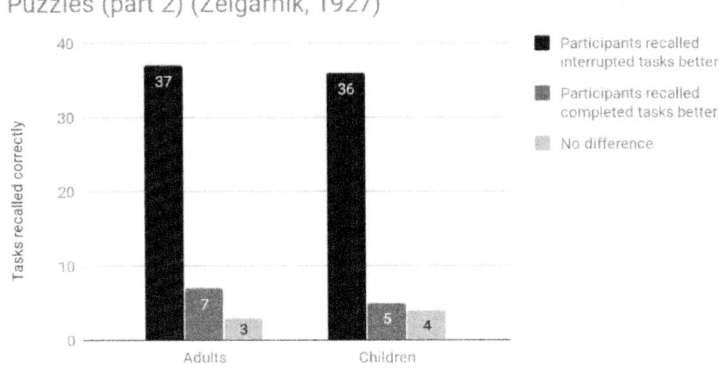

Of the forty-seven adults, thirty-seven remembered the interrupted task best, three remembered both equally well, seven recalled the completed ones best. Among the forty-five children, thirty-six were best in recalling unfinished tasks, four were equal, and five remembered the finished tasks best.

Individuals of all ages remember uncompleted tasks far better than completed ones.

Mazes (part 1)

Experiments have also been carried out to understand how long incomplete tasks remain in memory. In one experiment, forty-four participants were split into two groups and each trained to complete a simple maze (seven dead ends) without making any errors (McKinney, 1935).

One-half of the participants were told to learn the maze to three perfect repetitions without error. The others were told to perform just one perfect repetition. Both groups were stopped after they had made one perfect repetition. As such, the group that had been told that the maze must be completed without error three times believed they had been interrupted before the task had been completed.

Exactly twenty-four hours later, the participants were asked to recall the maze. The number of errors made by each participant was recorded.

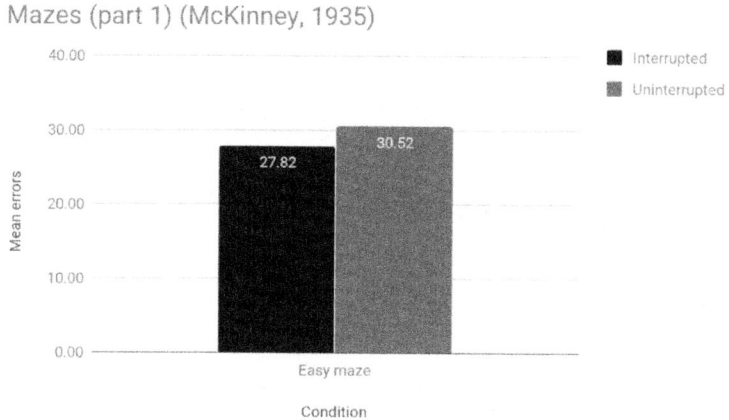

Mazes (part 1) (McKinney, 1935)

The uninterrupted group, on average, made three more errors than those who were interrupted before they could complete three perfect repetitions during the learning phase twenty-four hours earlier.

Again, the results suggest we still remember incomplete tasks better than those that have been completed, even twenty-four hours afterwards.

Mazes (part 2)

The researchers wondered whether the difference in recall between finished and unfinished tasks could extend beyond one week. As before, they split one hundred participants into two groups and trained them to complete a maze without any errors (McKinney, 1935). This time two mazes were used, one easy (seven dead ends) and one hard (ten dead ends).

One group of participants were told to learn the maze they were given, either hard or easy, to three perfect repetitions without error. The others were told to perform just one perfect repetition. Again, both groups were stopped after they had made one perfect repetition.

This time, participants were asked to complete the maze again exactly one week (seven days) later.

Mazes (part 2) (McKinney, 1935)

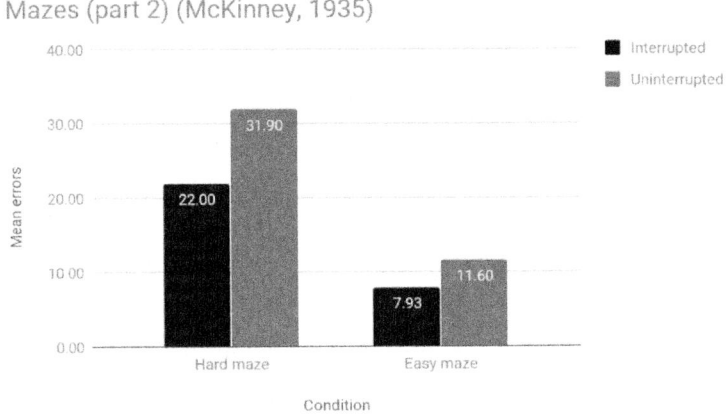

As expected, those recalling the hard maze one week later made more errors than those recalling the easy maze.

What's really interesting is that participants that were interrupted before they could complete three perfect repetitions during the learning phase a week earlier made fewer errors in both mazes. For the hard maze, the interrupted participants made an average of 22.00

mistakes compared to 31.90 mistakes for those who were interrupted.

Even over long periods of time, there is an increase in our ability to recall interrupted tasks better than completed tasks. The participants who were interrupted made far fewer errors than those that had completed the tasks one week later.

Mazes (part 3)

The researchers then hypothesised how the degree of completion, or mastery of a task, affected cognitive recall. In a similar experiment to the first maze experiment (part 1), forty-four participants were trained to complete a simple maze (seven dead ends) without making any errors (McKinney, 1935).

The difference in this experiment was that during their time learning the maze the interruption was introduced after varying levels of mastery. Some were stopped when they had managed to complete the maze with four errors each time, others when they were making only one error. The remaining participants were allowed to complete the task uninterrupted.

On the following day, twenty-four hours later, participants returned to recall the maze they had learned.

Mazes (part 3) (McKinney, 1935)

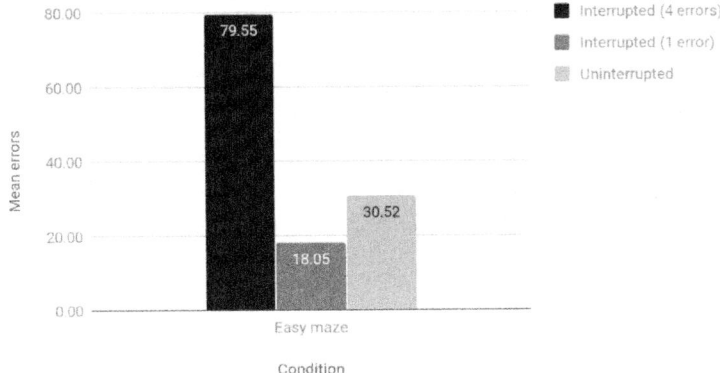

Fewer errors were made when participants had nearly mastered the task (at one error) during the learning phase the previous day (M = 18.05) than those that were allowed to learn the task completely uninterrupted (M = 30.52). However, the participants that had managed to complete the maze making four errors each time during the learning phase made significantly more errors than both groups (M = 79.55).

This study shows that an interruption in learning nearer the completion of the task is more effective in producing greater recall of that learning task itself. We are better at recalling details from tasks we are closer to mastering.

Jigsaw Puzzles

In the real world, especially at work, tasks often carry some level of stress. To test how stress changes the power of the effect, researchers set up an experiment. Participants were split into two groups and given jigsaw puzzles with pictures of everyday objects; a boat, a house, a bunch of grapes, for example (Rosenzweig, 2011).

One-half of the participants were told they would be evaluating the jigsaws for a future study, and were explicitly told it would not be a test of their own ability. They were also forewarned that they might be interrupted if the person running the experiment had "learned what they needed".

The second half of the participants were told they had been specially selected to take part in the study. Unlike the first group, this time the experiment was presented as a test of their own ability (an "intelligence-test"), with each participant being scored. Participants were warned they would be interrupted and stopped if they did not complete a puzzle within the time allocated.

All participants were permitted to finish half of the puzzles but were interrupted while working on the remaining half. The order of interruption varied for each participant. They were then requested to name the problems which they had attempted.

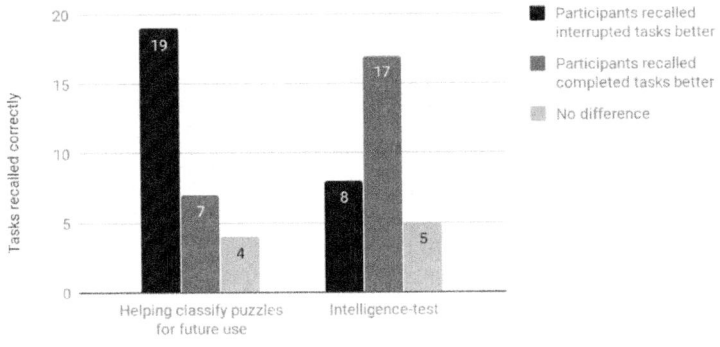

Jigsaw Puzzles (Rosenzweig, 2011)

The first group carrying out non-threatening, non-stressful tasks (helping classify puzzles for future use) recalled the unfinished tasks better than the finished ones (nineteen remembered more unfinished than finished tasks, seven did the opposite, while four recalled the same number of finished and unfinished tasks).

The individuals in the "intelligence test" group, who were presumably motivated to protect their egos, recalled finished tasks more frequently than unfinished ones (eight remembered more unfinished than finished tasks, seventeen did the opposite, while five recalled the same number of finished and unfinished tasks).

This study suggests threatening and stressful tasks that affect our self-esteem or pride cause us to remember details differently. We tend to remember our successes and forget unpleasant failures in such situations.

Product Gems

1. **Break down consumed content into smaller parts**
   Make content easier to digest. For example, create clear segments during a meeting to increase what attendees remember. This is especially powerful during product demos where engagement is key.
2. **Encourage temporary distractions**
   The Zeigarnik effect suggests that students who temporarily stop their studies, during which they do unrelated activities (such as studying unrelated participants or playing games), will remember material better than students who complete study sessions without a break.
3. **Think about self-esteem and ego**
   After having completed the task, are there things they'd be more likely, able or mentally free to do at the end of the task that they'd not be able to do prior to completion? Highlight their success in completing a task—perhaps installing a trial of your software product—and encourage them onto the next task.
4. **I've started, so I'll finish**
   If you're likely to procrastinate because you're faced with a big project, then don't think about starting with the hardest chunk of work. Start with what seems manageable at that moment. You'll be more likely to finish the task simply because you started. The Zeigarnik effect shows us that the key to beating procrastination is starting somewhere— anywhere (see: goal-gradient effect).
5. **Maintain intrigue**
   If you're looking to promote further consumption of material you're writing, focus on it being

incomplete, such as the use of an ellipsis instead of a full stop in an email header. Our natural desire to complete a task will result in the deeper content being read. Don't disclose all of the value of your work right at the beginning.

5. Nostalgia Effect

Thinking about the past makes us want to pay more now

Reminiscing about the past can make us spend more on products and services. Nostalgia weakens our desire to hold onto our money, instead fostering social connectedness.

Nostalgia marketing is the advertising equivalent of comfort food.

In a time when most marketing focuses heavily on the future, nostalgia transports us back to a simpler place where our current problems don't matter, and the hustle and bustle of modernity just melts away. Instead of anticipating the next great thing, nostalgia marketing urges us to focus on the things we already know are great.

We know at a gut level that nostalgia gives our lives a feeling of meaning and continuity. Nostalgia fulfils the need to belong and heightens feelings of social connectedness. When thinking back to past experiences of childhood I remember, nostalgically, long summer days and good friends from school.

Nostalgia mostly entails the recollection of a fond, meaningful memory. Individuals often reflect on the memory through rose-coloured glasses and may miss that time or person (Hepper et al., 2012). Individuals are likely to feel sentimental, tender, or happy, and often with a tinge of longing, believing "things were better in the past".

These dreamy feelings of a time-gone-by have been utilised by marketers and advertisers for some time because they leave us associating brands with a positive feeling. New research now suggests nostalgia also has a heightened effect on our willingness to spend on consumer goods and services.

The implications for the nostalgia effect are far-reaching for marketers, as well as for policymakers, and charitable and political organisations.

Super Bowl 2018

Television advertisement slots during the 2018 Super Bowl football game commanded $5 million for a 30-second slot, about $170k a second. Those figures ignore the millions that advertisers spend crafting an advertisement that will play a role as crucial as the football game for some consumers.

In the first three quarters of 2017, PepsiCo's soda volumes in the U.S. and Canada fell 4%. PepsiCo saw its soda brands sales slip partly because it shifted too much of its marketing firepower to its healthier drinks. That's where the company's 2018 Super Bowl advertisement came in.

Titled "This Is the Pepsi," the 30-second commercial featured celebrities that have been part of Pepsi's marketing in the past, including a new take on Cindy Crawford's famous Super Bowl ad from 1992. The advert was part of the company's wider "Pepsi Generation" campaign that had a running theme of nostalgia.

Nostalgia is such a powerful force in advertising Coca-Cola, Kia, and even a continent, Australia, with its ambitious remounting of the 1986 film Crocodile Dundee, ran adverts showing a time gone by during the 2018 Super Bowl.

The adverts were targeting many now well into adulthood who have nostalgic memories of a time gone by, times they want to replicate again, perhaps, in part, by purchasing a bottle of Pepsi (or Coca-Cola!).

Kodak Moments

Given that the experience of nostalgia can be tinged with longing for past relationships, researchers believed not only do we want to relive such experiences but would also be willing to pay more do so (Lasaleta et al., 2014).

To test this hypothesis, they set up an experiment where participants were shown a catalogue that contained an advertisement that promoted the same product, used the same (Kodak) branding and displayed the same photo.

Though two versions of the text below the advert were used, the participants were split in half and shown one of the two variations:

1. In the nostalgia condition, the copy read; "Remember special occasions with others from your past. Take a moment to cherish your childhood memories."
2. In the neutral condition, the copy read; "A special occasion with others. Think about making new memories starting today and well into your future."

All participants were then presented with the same booklet showing names and pictures of 24 products and reported their willingness to pay for each. The products ranged from high-end (e.g., house) to midrange (e.g., sweatshirt) to low-end (e.g., a 1-litre bottle of Coke).

Kodak Moments (Lasaleta et al., 2014)

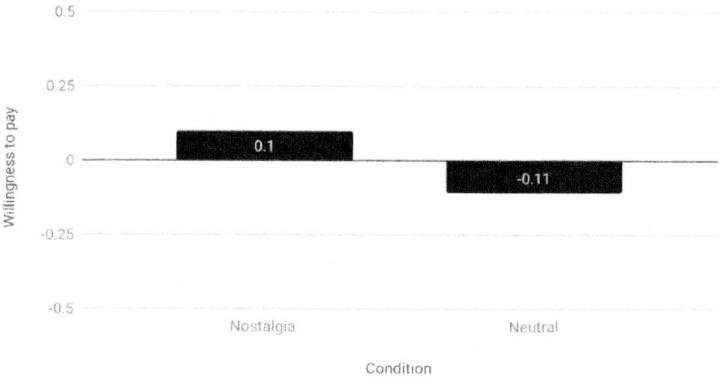

Given that average willingness to pay varied as a function of product from $1.67 (1-litre bottle of Coke) to $292,671.43 (house), researchers standardised willingness-to-pay scores.

Willingness to pay for participants in the nostalgic memory condition was higher (M = 0.1) than in the neutral condition (M = -0.11).

Advertisements that prompt us to think about nostalgic memories, compared to those that prompt us to think about making new memories, make us more willing to pay more for products -- even if they're not those being advertised.

Half the Sky Foundation

Prosocial behaviour can affect the way we assess products (see: Prosocial Effect). As demonstrated in the previous experiment, nostalgia weakens our desire to hold onto money something that could aid in raising the number and volume of charitable donations.

To test this idea, a group of researchers conducted an experiment using an appeal for a fictional charity (Zhou et al. 2012), Half the Sky Foundation. This appeal either contained nostalgic cues (nostalgic appeal condition) or did not contain nostalgic cues (neutral appeal condition).

To assess charitable giving, a collection box for the charity was placed near the exit of the room. The amount of money that participants placed in the box served as an index of charitable giving. I should note, all the money was returned to each participant following the experiment.

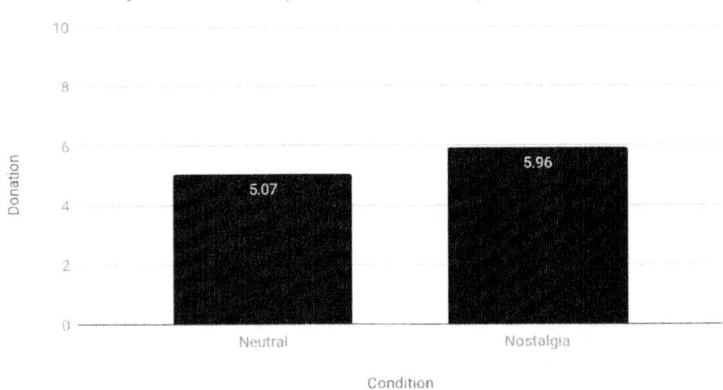

Half the Sky Foundation (Zhou et al., 2012)

The results were consistent with the hypothesis. Participants who were exposed to the nostalgic appeal contributed more money (M = 5.96) than did participants exposed to the non-nostalgic appeal (M = 5.07).

Nostalgic appeals are especially effective to increase tangible charitable behaviour by raising the average donation given by an individual.

Dictator Game

In both the Kodak Moment and Half the Sky Foundation experiments it is clear that nostalgia increased the valuation of products, which was reflected in higher willingness-to-pay scores. In a follow-up experiment, researchers wanted to further test this hypothesis on other resources, specifically time (Lasaleta et al., 2014).

The experiment used the Dictator game, in which one player, the dictator, gets to decide how much of an initial sum of money (say, $10) they would like to give to the second player. The dictator then keeps the remaining sum of money. Economic theory predicts that the dictator will always make the most self-interested choice.

Before the game began, participants were split into two groups:

1. In the nostalgic condition, the participants were asked to write about a time they felt nostalgic.
2. In the neutral condition, participants were asked neutral condition and instructed them to write about an ordinary event from their past.

In the game, the two groups of participants were endowed with one of two resources: time or money. The game was described to them as having two players, a receiver and a proposer, the latter of whom was granted an endowment of money or time.

In the money resource condition, participants had the option of allocating money, in 19, $0.25 increments, to the receiver. In the time-resource condition, participants could divide

19 units of 30 seconds between the two parties. The time each participant was given would allow them to leave the experiment early by that amount.

Dictator Game (Lasaleta et al., 2014)

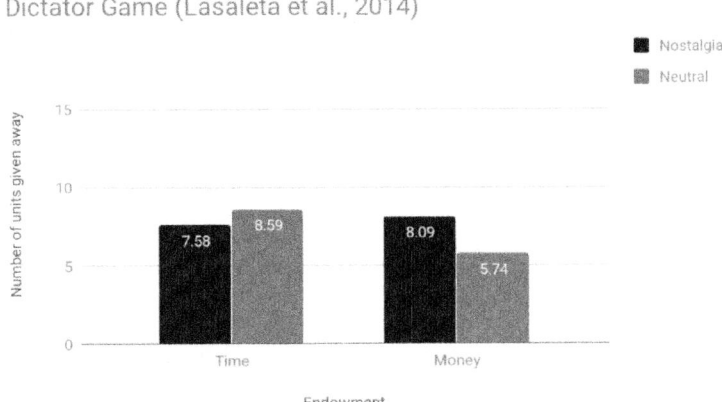

In the money dictator game, nostalgic event participants gave significantly more resource units away compared to those in the ordinary past event condition (M = 8.09 vs M = 5.74, respectively). However, in the time dictator game, there was no difference in resource allocation between nostalgic and ordinary event participants (M = 7.58 vs M = 8.59, respectively).

Participants who had recalled a nostalgic event gave away more money, but not time, than those who had recently recalled an ordinary past life event. Nostalgia participants allocated 42% of their money (8.09 units), approximately 40% more money than those in the neutral condition, indicating a weakened desire to hold onto their money.

Not all factors are equal when it comes to nostalgia. Nostalgia causes us to render money to be less desirable to hold on to, or put another way, more

willing to spend it, but this is not true of our time, something service-based products should be aware of.

For example, nostalgia won't always help if you're trying to get people to spend a morning at your event (though it might increase the amount they're willing to spend if they do want to attend!).

Ex-Presidents

On the 2008 U.S. presidential election day the polling organisation, Gallup, ran a poll asking participants to select from five ex-presidents who, in theory, they thought would best serve as the next U.S. president (Saad, 2008).

Each participant was first shown a list of five ex-presidents; Abraham Lincoln, Franklin Roosevelt, John F. Kennedy, Ronald Reagan, and Bill Clinton. After seeing the presidents in the list, they were asked to select their preference to serve as the next U.S president.

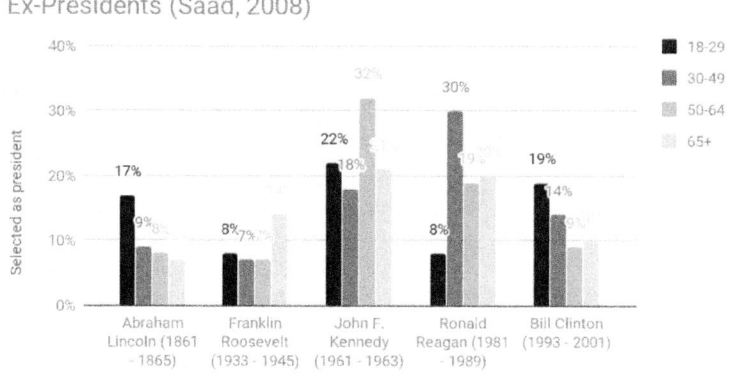

Ex-Presidents (Saad, 2008)

Nostalgia appears to play a modest role in Americans' choice of past president to serve the country today. The most popular choice of Baby Boomers, now aged about 50 to 64, is the man who was president of their youth: Kennedy (M = 32%). The top choice of those 30 to 49 years of age (broadly speaking, Generation X) is the president who served during their childhood or young adult years: Reagan (30%).

Nostalgia has powerful effects on our decisions across our lifetimes. Not only does it directly impact our wallet but also our longstanding thoughts, decisions and beliefs.

Holiday Season

Time is also an important factor in our decisions though. A craving for nostalgia has been especially strong since the financial crisis of 2008, but that does not mean that nostalgia is only relevant during a finite period. There are times of the
year when people may be particularly prone to nostalgia, such as the winter holiday season.

Researchers tested the idea that people long for objects, others, and times from the past more during the holiday season compared to other periods of the year (Lasaleta et al., 2014).

Some participants completed Batcho's (1995) Nostalgia Inventory during the 2009 Christmas holiday season whereas others completed it during the third week of January 2010.

The Nostalgia Inventory is a 20-item scale that captures to the extent to which people miss objects, people, experiences, and places from the past. The inventory required participants to "Rate how much you miss each of the items listed below" from 1 (not at all) to 5 (very much). Items included "family", "not having to worry," and "toys".

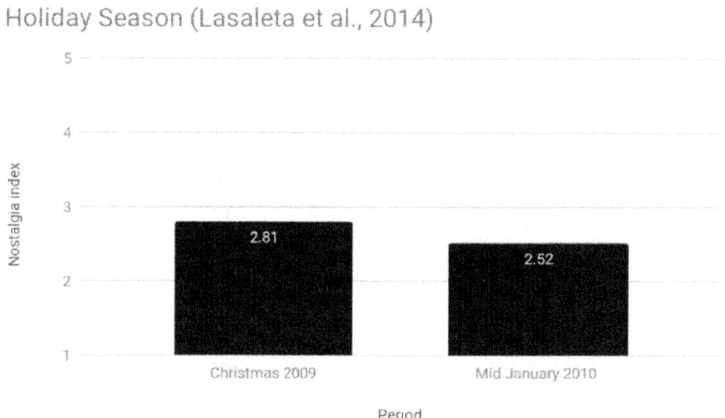

Holiday Season (Lasaleta et al., 2014)

The participants reported being more nostalgic during the Christmas holiday season compared (M = 2.81) to mid-January (M = 2.52).

The periodicities in nostalgic feelings often are—not coincidentally—tied to heightened consumer spending.

Product Gems

1. **Understand the past deeply affects the future**
   Consumers' nostalgia for the past can have a powerful and long-lasting effect on their decisions. This is particularly important when you're trying to change a consumer's long-held behaviour or habit (or who they're going to vote for).

2. **Use to combat price sensitivity**
   For marketers, the findings suggest feeling nostalgic could decrease consumer price sensitivity. In highly competitive environments introducing nostalgia can be used to alleviate pricing concerns.

3. **Make it timely**
   There are times of the year when people may be particularly prone to nostalgia. Economic periods can have the same effect too. In times of recession, when consumers are reluctant to part with their money, nostalgia could be used to help stimulate a dwindling economy, which may be one reason why nostalgia-themed promotions and products have been so popular in the years following the 2008 financial crisis (Elliot, 2009).

4. **Think about the age of your consumers**
   Nostalgia experiences differ with age. My grandparents talk about what life used to be like differ from my parents, which differ from mine. Make sure you're aware of the nostalgia your consumers long for.

5. **It's about social connectedness**
   Nostalgia fulfils the need to belong and heightens feelings of social connectedness. These findings may provide a reason why the elderly are particularly sensitive to nostalgic marketing

because social relationships tend to decrease as we age. In a similar manner, it also explains why older people are more at risk for financial scams (Repa, 2013), as an increased propensity for nostalgia may result in a weaker hold on their money.

6. **Create products around the theme of nostalgia**
Clearly, this effect has implications for "social" products and services like social networking sites with users seeking connectedness. If you are trying to improve consumer loyalty, find ways to foster a sense of social connectedness by helping to build and maintain long-term social relationships. Example: Timehop.

7. **Use nostalgia to promote good nudges too**
Putting consumers in a nostalgic state can promote prosocial behaviour, such as donating to charity, as they will be more receptive to parting with their money. Research has also shown for prosocial activities that nostalgia might weaken our desire to hold onto other resources too. When faced with self-interested, we're less willing to give up time when in a nostalgic state, however, in non-self-interested scenarios, such as volunteering, consumers actually are much more willing to part with their time for a good cause (Zhou et al., 2012).

6. Lucky Loyalty Effect

The more we spend, the luckier we feel

Loyal consumers' have a greater sense of deservedness. The more consumers invest in your brand, the more they incorrectly believe that they'll win entirely random promotions over less loyal customers.

Loyalty programs are becoming increasingly common. My local supermarket sends me vouchers at the end of each month, the airline I fly with occasionally grants me upgrades, and I can earn a free coffee after buying ten from my favourite coffee shop.

Consumers know there are benefits that come with loyalty, even when loyalty programs are not in place. A loyal customer of ten years is likely to expect a bigger discount compared to a new customer when their contract comes up for renewal.

The lucky loyalty effect is a powerful tool to motivate loyal spenders into engaging with your promotions. Though beware, consumers believe that if they're loyal, they'll get treated better than "normal" customers, with hierarchies based on prior spending separating and enhancing levels of satisfaction.

Hotel Loyalty

As an important decision maker, you might have to travel frequently. When on the road you always try to book a hotel room at a hotel chain you're particularly loyal too. As a result, you're fairly high up in their loyalty programme, and you get room upgrades every so often.

Imagine it's the off-season and the hotel chain are running a promotional campaign: every 100th booking made on their website will be completely free.

Aware of this campaign, you, the privileged and loyal customer make your booking on their website and lo and behold, your confirmation comes back with something special—you've somehow bagged the free booking!

Don't forget that the chance of winning this promotion was entirely random and had absolutely nothing to do with your level of spending. Despite this, you might believe you had a greater chance of winning due to your loyalty to the hotel chain compared to other customers. If you hadn't won, you might have questioned why you didn't.

Consumers believe that they're more likely to win a promotion, the more they spend with that company.

Hotel Gift Basket

In an experiment studying the lucky loyalty effect, 197 participants were asked to imagine checking into a 500-room hotel for a two-night stay (Reczek et al., 2014).

The participants were split into two groups. The first group was told to imagine they were a loyal customer of the hotel brand. The second group was told the opposite; to imagine this was the first time staying at a hotel operated by the hotel brand.

All were then asked to read an announcement that there would be a daily random drawing for one guest room to receive a special gift basket of cheese, crackers, fruit wine and other gourmet foods. Importantly, they were also told that all guests would be automatically entered into the random draw for the prize.

Participants were then asked how likely, from 1 (strongly disagree) to 7 (strongly agree), they were to win the gift basket compared to other guests.

Hotel Gift Basket (Reczek et al., 2014)

The loyal customers felt luckier, estimating their chances of winning the gift basket to be higher than the new customers (M = 2.91 vs M = 2.39).

People felt more likely to win a company promotion when they were loyal and had invested in the brand.

Credit Card Rewards

The researchers realised this first experiment mixed together spending and status into one (as is normal in the real world). A second experiment aimed to pick these two apart and see which was really responsible for the lucky loyalty effect (Reczek et al., 2014).

This time 222 people were asked to imagine that a clothing retailer with which they held a store credit card sent out discount coupons—between 5-30% off any purchase, in 5% increments—to cardholders once every six months. They were also informed there were far more 5% discounts available than 30% discounts, and that the discount they'd receive would be entirely random.

They were split into four groups, separated by elite status (Most valuable customer / not) and prior spending (more than $1000 / none). They were then asked to rate, from 1 (strongly disagree) to 7 (strongly agree), how much they agreed with the following statement:

"I am likely to receive a higher level of discount than other customers who have a credit card with this store."

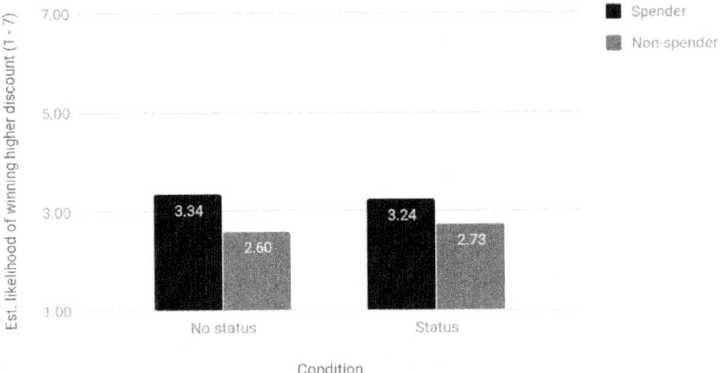

Credit Card Rewards (Reczek et al., 2014)

The previous spenders in both status and no status groups both estimated their likelihood of receiving the higher discounts to be roughly equal, M = 3.34 and M = 3.24 respectively, as did those who had any spent money at the store previously, M = 2.60 and M = 2.73. When looking at spenders versus non-spenders, the results get interesting. Those asked to imagine spending over $1000 at the store previously believed they were much likely to receive higher rewards than others, even though they had no knowledge of what other consumers had spent previously.

The results show that prior spending is the important factor here. Status alone doesn't produce the lucky loyalty effect, but spending (effort) does.

Online Shopping (part 1)

Researchers also wanted to test how a person's effort, in this case, the amount of money spent, affected the power of the lucky loyalty effect. This time, ninety-nine participants were told to imagine receiving an email that contained a discount code from an online retailer (Reczek et al., 2014).

The participants were split into two groups. The first group was told to imagine they had spent over $1000 with the retailer in the past six months. The second group was told they had spent less than $20 in the previous six months.

Similar to before, participants were told to rate, from 1 (strongly disagree) to 7 (strongly agree), how much they believed they were likely to receive a higher discount than other customers of the online store.

Online shopping (part 1) (Reczek et al., 2014)

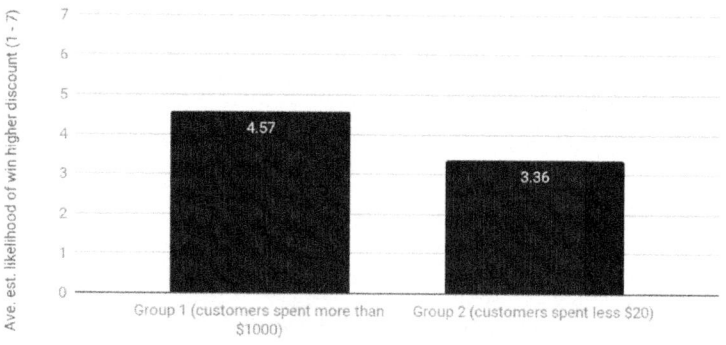

Again, the experiment demonstrated the lucky loyalty effect in full effect. The participants asked to imagine they had spent more previously at the store believed they had a better chance of receiving the highest discounts (M = 4.57) compared to other customers (M = 3.36), **even when they were unaware how much the other customers had spent. Or put another way, how much money they had spent compared others.**

Online Shopping (part 2)

Researchers then wanted to better understand how participants compared their effort versus the likelihood of winning a reward compared to others when they were aware of the "average customer" by prior spend.

In total, 232 participants were asked to read the same scenario about a retailer emailing discount codes to cardholders (Reczek et al., 2014). Participants were split into two groups, separated by prior spending (more than $1000 / none).

They were then asked to compare, from 1 (strongly disagree) to 7 (strongly agree), how much they agreed with the following two statements:

1. *"I am more likely to receive a 30% discount code than other credit card holders who have spent $20 or less in the last six months."*
2. *"I am more likely to receive a 30% discount code than other credit card holders who have spent $1000 or more in the last six months."*

Online shopping (part 2) (Reczek et al., 2014)

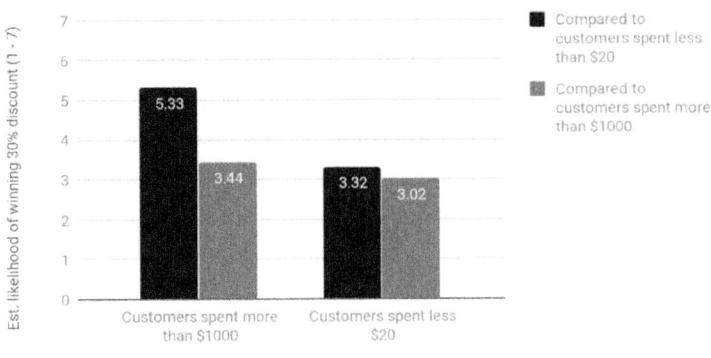

Those asked to imagine they had spent $1000 previously believed they were far more likely to win the 30% discount over those who had spent less than $20 (M = 5.33). When comparing the likelihood of receiving the discount over others who had also spent large amounts with the online store, their estimated likelihood of receiving the discount was much lower (M = 3.44).

On the other hand, participants asked to imagine spending less than $20 believed they had a slightly lower chance of receiving the discount when comparing themselves to other customers spending $20 (M = 3.32), but only slightly less when comparing themselves to customers spending $1000 (M = 3.02).

Consumers have a tendency to believe their luck is greater only when they're comparing themselves against the general consumer, not other similarly loyal folks.

Product Gems

1. **Loyal customers expect special treatment**
   It all comes down to a sense of entitlement. The more consistent consumers are with their actions (spending with a hotel chain, for instance), the higher the level of deservingness they feel. So, if they are already used to being rewarded for past effort, customers can create an unrealistic expectation that future efforts will also be rewarded. Be cautious you do not alienate this group of customers.

2. **Status isn't everything**
   Remember, it's prior spending and not status alone that influences a feeling of luck for your loyal customers. The fundamental reason for this is that as we spend more, we feel we deserve more in return. Think about using a points-based loyalty scheme directly linked to how much a customer has spent alongside status tiers (see: goal-gradient effect).

3. **Use creatively in promotions**
   Think about ways you could increase a customer's effort, perhaps increasing average spend, to increase their sense of "luck". Out in the field, Kohl's, a US department store, has had a significant degree of success with its recent random reward promotional campaign called Dream Receipts. Here, one random customer in each store each day has their shopping paid for them by the store. In this instance, the customer's average spend increased for two key reasons; they believed by spending more their chances of winning or "luck" increased (even though a single receipt was effectively worth one entry to the raffle), but also

that the reward (the amount they stood to win) would be greater the more they purchased.

4. **Set expectations**

   Customers who believe they have exerted no more effort than the "average" consumer will not feel the sense of luck the effect brings. Make sure your customers know where they fit in your customer base. Airlines are particularly good at this through their very public marketing of a customer's tier status (priority boarding, special luggage tags, free upgrades, etc.)

5. **Higher spenders will be more receptive**

   Higher spending customers will be more likely to engage with promotions, given their higher expected probability of winning. Other research shows that those who've invested both the most and the least within your loyalty program prefer riskier, larger rewards (Kivetz & Simonson, 2003). Focus your promotional spend accordingly.

6. **But include everyone in promotions**

   When designing your promotional campaigns, remember to include a broad spectrum of your customer base. Including (or appearing to just include) only your "most-valued" customers will reduce their feeling of luck, reducing engagement. Instead of entering only top-tier customers into the promotion, inform your customers that they all have a chance to win.

7. **Keep it brand focused**

   Make sure that any promotions are directly tied to your brand and not a partnership with another company. Activities outside of your brand will weaken the lucky loyalty effect. For example, asking your customers to "Like" your brand on

Facebook will not foster the same sense of luck (Reczek et al., 2014).

8. **It works on employees too**

Your employees put effort into your company; closed sales, research and development, and manufacturing are good examples. As discussed, the lucky loyalty effect can be used to further increase their productivity as they try to increase their chance of winning random rewards. Beware; if you give out rewards in search of motivating your employees, remember that those who don't win might feel resentment. Try to foster a healthy sense of competition rather than in-fighting.

7. Sunk Cost Fallacy

We're reluctant to pull out of something we have already put effort into

The prospect of losses is a more powerful motivator on our behaviour than the promise of gains. When we put time and effort into something, we're motivated to make it work. We therefore often continue to invest in it, even if it brings us losses.

The chances are that even if you pride yourself on being rational most of the time, you will still occasionally fall victim to the sunk cost fallacy. As an emotional human, your aversion to loss often leaves you helpless to avoid it. Do any of these examples sound familiar?

"I might as well keep eating because I already bought the food."
"I might as well continue to pump money into a failing business idea because I've been working on it for a whole year."
"Even though I feel unwell, I will go to the cinema tonight because I've already paid for the tickets."

Sunk costs are a favourite subject of economists. Simply put, they are payments or investments which can never be recovered. The sunk cost fallacy is a great example of our past efforts influencing our current and future decisions.

Your decisions are tainted by the emotional investments you accumulate, and the more you invest in something, the harder it becomes to abandon it.

Farmville

You've probably heard of the game, Farmville. In 2010, one in five Facebook users had a Farmville account. For those that haven't played the game, the sheer numbers alone suggest it is a really fun game. Actually, the lasting appeal of Farmville has little to do with fun.

The basic premise of the game is to build and maintain a farm, from planting seeds to looking after livestock. When you first begin, you have just enough money to buy some basic crops. As the game progresses, you earn more virtual money and invest in ever more expensive virtual farm items; for example, a tractor or a new barn.

This is the powerful force behind Farmville. Playing Farmville is a commitment to virtual life. Your neglect has consequences. You must return, sometimes days later, to reap the reward of the time and virtual money you are spending now. If you don't return, your investments die, and you will feel like you wasted your time, money and effort.

Players continue to play, not to have fun, but to avoid negative emotions. They can never get back the time or the money they've spent, but they keep playing to avoid feeling the pain of loss and the ugly sensation waste creates.

Ski Trip

Psychologist Hal Arkes and partner Catherine Blumer suggest that sunk costs may dissuade you from choosing "fun" when it is an option.

Researchers at Ohio University asked sixty-one college students to assume that, by mistake, they had purchased tickets for a $50 ski trip to Wisconsin and a $100 ski trip to Michigan, for the same weekend (Arkes & Blumer, 1985).

The students were told they would have much more fun on the $50 trip to Wisconsin than the $100 trip to Michigan. They were then asked to choose one of the trips and let the ticket for the other go to waste.

Ski Trip (Arkes & Blumer, 1985)

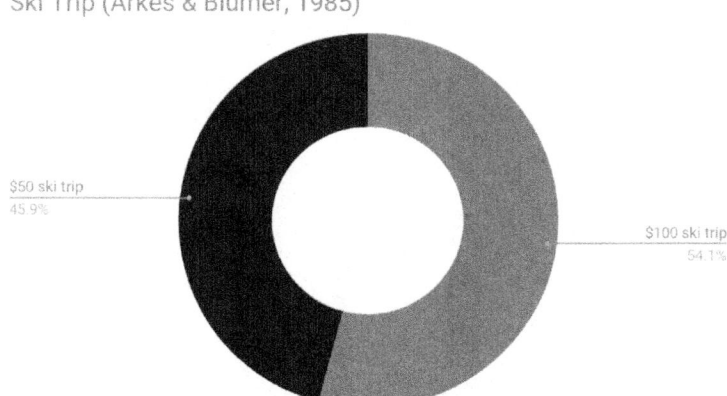

$50 ski trip
45.9%

$100 ski trip
54.1%

Perhaps surprisingly, the majority of students, 54.1% (33 of 61), chose the less enjoyable $100 trip. It seems the higher sunk cost represented by the $100 payment was more important to them than getting greater enjoyment from the less expensive $50 trip that they had paid for.

We don't treat losses and gains equally. We're more willing to give up a more positive experience to account for a larger cost that we've incurred.

Theatre Tickets

In another experiment conducted by Arkes and Blumer, sixty participants were offered various priced tickets to a local theatre (Arkes & Blumer, 1985). Some were offered tickets at full price ($15), some were offered tickets with a $2 discount, and others were offered tickets with a $7 discount.

Each ticket would allow the participant to attend as many plays as they wished for the whole year. The researchers divided the year into two halves; the first five plays and the last five plays.

Theatre Tickets (Arkes & Blumer, 1985)

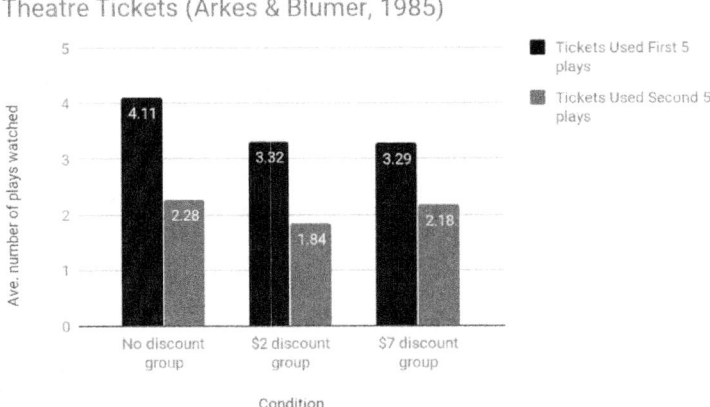

Those who had purchased theatre tickets at the full-price used more theatre tickets (M = 4.11) for the first five plays than those who purchased tickets at either of the two discounted prices (M = 3.32 and M = 3.29 for $2 and $7, respectively).

Interestingly, during the second five plays, there was little difference in the use of tickets, suggesting our perceived losses of a sunk cost decrease over time.

Car Usage

In one study examining real-world examples of the sunk cost fallacy, researchers in Singapore analysed the purchases of 7398 middle-value cars between 2001-2011 (Ho et al., 2013).

During this period, the sunk costs involved in a new car purchase varied significantly due to changes in government taxation. For example, from 2009 to 2010, new vehicle taxes increased by $4500 SGD, the equivalent of $3500 USD at the time.

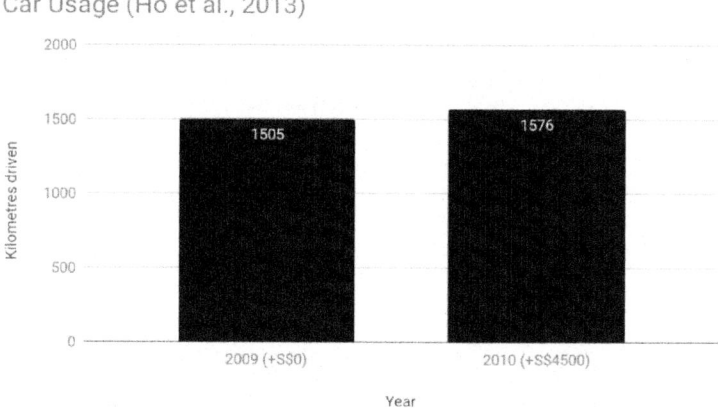

Car Usage (Ho et al., 2013)

An increase in the sunk cost by $4,500 SGD led to an increase in monthly car usage by 70.9 kilometres or 4.5% in the first four years of ownership. Over the whole four years, that adds up to an additional 3,403 kilometres driven.

The money paid to the government could not be recovered, it was sunk—owners could not recover this money if they sold the car to someone else. The sunk costs should not affect the number of miles we drive, or how much we utilise a something, however, this experiment suggests differently.

We better utilise products and services with a higher sunk cost.

Chocolate Stand

When money is involved, our brains are always working hard to avoid losses. When a free product is introduced, it can turn off our brain's loss aversion systems.

In an experiment designed to test this theory, researchers offered 398 people the opportunity to purchase chocolates from a stand they had set up (Ariely et al., 2007). There were two choices available: Hershey's Kisses for $0.01 each or Lindt Truffles for $0.15 each (condition 1). It is important to point out the Lindt Truffles are generally regarded to be made of much higher quality chocolate and are sold in shops at a much higher price than Hershey's Kisses.

The researchers then set up another booth with the same two choices but lowered the price of each chocolate by $0.01; Hershey's Kisses for $0.00 (free) each or Lindt Truffles for $0.14 each (condition 2).

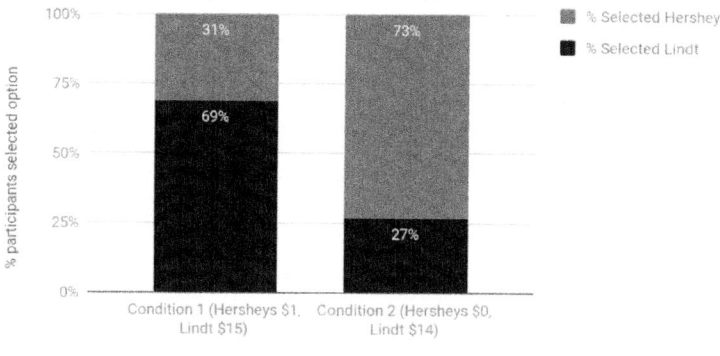

Chocolate Stand (Ariely et al., 2007)

For the first part of the experiment (condition 1), the majority of people who faced this offer chose the Lindt Truffles (69%) because they appeared to be a good deal considering the quality differences and the normal prices of both chocolates.

When both chocolates were reduced by just $0.01 (condition 2), with the Hershey's Kisses now costing $0.00, the vast majority of people selected the Hershey's Kisses (73%) instead of the truffles. If participants had acted on pure mathematical logic, there should have been no significant change in behaviour because the price reduction was the same. However, this wasn't the case.

The researchers suggested our loss-aversion systems remain inactive when there is a "free" option. You don't weigh the pros and cons with as much attention to detail as you would if you had to factor in potential financial losses.

We do not value something that is free on its cost-benefit differences because there is no perceived sunk cost.

Product Gems

1. **Sell the value**
   The sunk cost fallacy explains why marketing and good salesmanship is often all about convincing you that what you want to buy is worth more than what you must pay for it. You see something as good value when you predict the pain of loss will be offset by your joy of gain. When trying to sell to your customers, focus on the benefits they will receive, rather than a long list of irrelevant features.

2. **Then upsell**
   Informing customers of a cost that has already been incurred can help increase sales. For example, when customers put through an order for some trousers on an online store, along with the price, seeing a message that reads "complete the look with this black shirt for only $20" can dramatically increase average basket value. It does this by reminding customers how much they've already invested towards their overall clothing purchase and highlighting how small the extra sum required would be to 'complete the set' (which itself plays on our natural desire to complete things).

3. **Value highlighting to smooth out kinks**
   If, however, you're struggling with underutilisation or cancellations at the last minute, notify consumers in the run-up to an event of what they've pre-ordered and its value to increase the sunk cost fallacy and thus their desire to follow through.

4. **Reminding as a means of post-selling**
   Similar to value highlighting, sunk costs have a strong potential to increase the purchase of post-

sale consumables (such as antivirus software for a laptop or check-up services for durable goods).

5. **Not just monetary**

   The time and effort your prospects invest also produces a similar, if sometimes less powerful effect. One example of this is getting a prospect to commit to installing and configuring a trial version of your software product.

6. **Don't fall victim**

   Never be afraid to turn away from an opportunity that is not working out, no matter how much time and effort you've invested in it. The opportunity cost of other things— other deals, for example—could be significantly higher.

7. **Embrace the power of "free"**

   Offering free trials, free delivery, or free gifts can offset your customers' believed risk of paid products. Items offered free of charge are highly attractive because of their perceived value, compared to when they're offered at cost (see: endowment effect, next chapter).

8. Endowment Effect

We value something more once we feel we own it

People will tend to pay more to retain something they own than to obtain something they do not own—even when there is no cause for attachment, or even if the item was only obtained minutes ago.

Flying is relatively cheap these days. A round-trip from London to mainland Europe can, when timed correctly, cost less than a thirty-minute train ride in the UK. While browsing a travel website recently, I uncovered one such deal—a trip from London to Milan for around the price of a good meal at my favourite restaurant.

Even though I had not planned on returning to the city so soon, I'd visited the year before, the voice in the back of my mind made me click to read more about the offer. Not only was it a brilliant deal, reading beyond the normal terms and condition, it also noted the travel agent offered a free cancellation up to seven days before the flight departed.

The flights were six months away, and although only five minutes ago I had no plans for another visit, now my mindset was different, "What could I lose?" There was a five-month period in which to change my mind with no financial penalties. Needless to say, the tickets were booked, and as you probably guessed, I spent four days in Italy enjoying good weather, good food and good wine.

The endowment effect demonstrates that people place extra value on what they own. In effect, people demand more to give up an object they own than they are willing to pay for it. Not only does it catch out those booking flights with a money-back guarantee, but the endowment effect can also lead even the best decision makers to choose the suboptimal option because of familiarity and comfort.

Netflix

Many companies offer free trials; Amazon Prime for two-day shipping and Netflix for thirty days of free streaming. For both these companies, trial periods have been hugely successful. Take Netflix; the thirty-day trial period has been largely attributed to 100% growth in subscribers from 26.5 million to 57.4 million between 2012 and 2014.

Many customers, myself included, sign up for the free trial with the mindset to not continue the service and just take advantage of it while it is free. Though as the month comes to an end, and with a backlog of titles in a watchlist, Netflix's monthly fee now seems relatively cheap.

The perceived value of Netflix's service increases during the free trial, in large part due to the endowment effect. Subscribers tend to value the service much more highly once they own it and so are much less willing to give it up.

Raffle Tickets

Early studies of the endowment effect examined the differences in willingness to pay and willingness to accept for items. Seventy-six participants were randomly assigned raffle tickets that were one of two colours (Knetsch & Sinden, 1984). Each participant was told that the winner would receive a $70 voucher or, at the choice of the winner, $50 in cash.

Half of the participants, determined by the colour of their tickets, were asked to pay $2 to keep their ticket for the prize draw (payment). The other half of the participants were allowed to take part in the raffle without paying for their ticket, but they were each offered $2 to forgo their entry (compensation).

Raffle Tickets (Knetsch & Sinden, 1984)

Of the thirty-eight people offered the opportunity to pay $2 to participate in the raffle, nineteen participants paid for their ticket, while the other nineteen refused. Interestingly, of those offered to be paid $2 for their ticket before the raffle, twenty-nine refused and just nine accepted.

These results show that fewer people thought that the opportunity to participate was worth $2 when measured on the basis of willingness to pay than when measured on the basis of refusing compensation to give up the ticket they already owned.

Those who already owned a ticket valued it more highly than those who had to purchase one.

Coffee and Chocolate

Another group of researchers, intrigued by the experiment above, decided to further examine the endowment effect. They realised that the results of the first experiment might be influenced by risk, as the actual value of the lottery ticket was unknown—or put another way, whether it would be a winner.

In their first experiment, 218 participants were split into three groups; the first group were given a coffee mug sold at the bookstore of the University they attended, the second were given a common Swiss chocolate bar, the third-and-final group were given the option to choose either the mug or chocolate bar (Kahneman et al., 1991).

Both the coffee mug and chocolate bar were priced similarly in the bookstore.

Those in the first two groups were then asked if they would trade the item they were first endowed with for the other choice, either the coffee mug or chocolate bar.

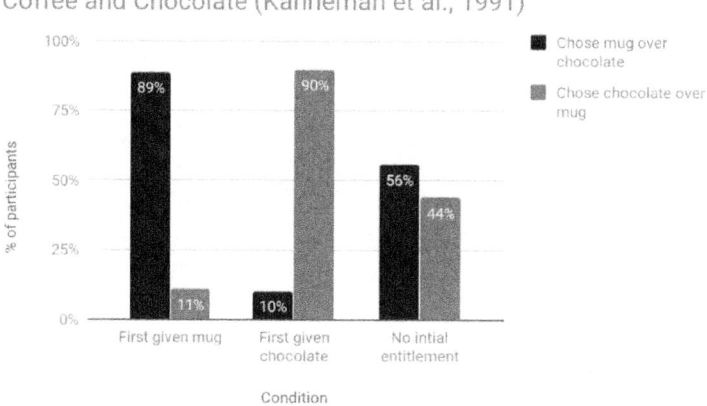

Coffee and Chocolate (Kahneman et al., 1991)

When given a choice, 56% of the participants selected the coffee mug over the chocolate bar, while 44% of participants chose the chocolate bar instead of the coffee mug. A fairly even split, as expected.

It gets really interesting when you look at the other two groups. When asked to exchange the coffee mug for an equally priced chocolate bar, only 11% accepted the trade, while the other 89% opted to keep the mug. Similarly, 90% of those given the chocolate bar kept hold of it, only 10% chose to trade it for the coffee mug.

Even after a short period of time, the endowment effect kicked in and participants valued the item they were endowed with over a similarly priced alternative.

Coffee Mug

In a follow-up experiment, seventy-seven participants were shown a coffee mug sold at the bookstore of the University they attended (Kahneman et al., 1991).

Next, the participants were split into three groups; the first group were given the mug asked if they would be willing to sell it at a series of prices ranging from $0.25 to $9.25 (sellers), the second group were asked about how much they would be willing to pay for the mug using the same price series (buyers), the third group were asked to choose between receiving the mug or the amount of money in cash for each of the prices (choosers).

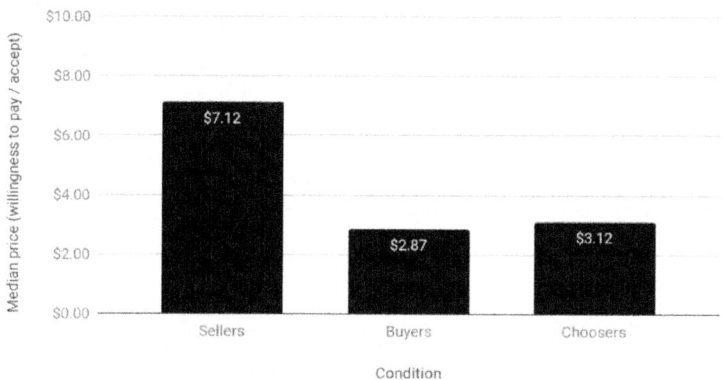

Coffee Mug (Kahneman et al., 1991)

In line with the previous experiments, those who owned the mug were only willing to accept a much higher amount to sell the mug (Md = $7.12) than buyers were willing to pay (Md = $2.87), over $4 more.

The allocation of a mug to the sellers evidently induced a sense of endowment that the buyers did not share, and the same outcome was observed in the chooser's group, too. The median value of the coffee mug to the sellers (Md = $7.12) was more than double the value indicated by the choosers (Md = $3.13) even though their choices, whether to keep the mug or take money, were objectively the same.

After analysing the results, researchers suggested that:

> **"the low volume of trade is produced mainly by owner's reluctance to part with their endowment, rather than by buyers' unwillingness to part with their cash."**

Basketball Tickets

In addition to coffee mugs and chocolate bars, the endowment effect has been observed using different goods and in a wide range of different populations (including monkeys!).

In one such experiment, ninety-three participants were interviewed about tickets to an upcoming basketball tournament, the NCAA Final Four (Carmon & Ariely, 2000). Each participant was first asked the highest price they would pay for a final game ticket. They were then told to imagine they owned a ticket to the final and were asked what the lowest price they would agree to sell it for would be.

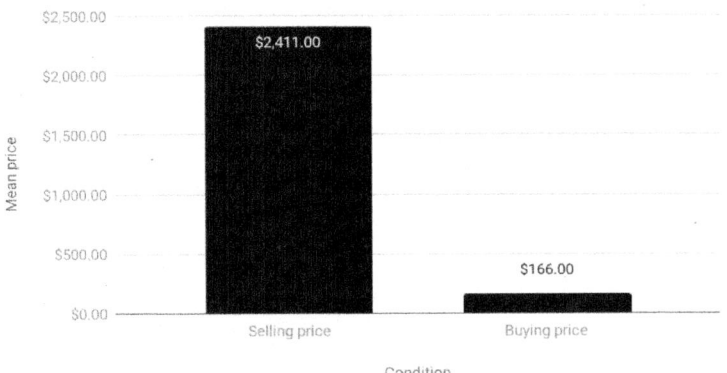

Basketball Tickets (Carmon & Ariely, 2000)

For those who have ever browsed resale ticket markets, the results will not be surprising. When asked how much they would be willing to accept to sell the tickets, participants valued them fourteen times higher (M = $2,411) than their hypothetical buying price (M = $166).

Buyers and sellers differ not simply in their valuation of the same item but also in how they assess the

value. Buyers tend to focus on their sentiment toward what they forgo (typically, the expenditure). By the same token, sellers tend to focus on their sentiment toward surrendering the item, and selling prices are hence more heavily influenced by variables such as the benefits of possessing the item.

Employee Bonuses

The endowment effect extends beyond the trading of goods and services. It can also influence productivity, as shown in the next experiment conducted with the help of a real business.

Wanlida Group, a high-tech Chinese enterprise engaged in the production and distribution of consumer electronics employs over 20,000 people. The company agreed to allow researchers to test how different bonus schemes affected productivity with a subset of their employees (List & Hossain, 2009).

One group of employees were told that they would receive a bonus of 80 yuan (approximately $12 at the time) at the end of the week if they met a given production target (the prospect of gain). Another group were told that they had provisionally been awarded the same bonus, also paid at the end of the week, but that they would lose it if their productivity fell short of the same threshold (the prospect of loss). Objectively these are two ways of describing the same scheme.

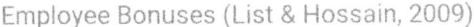

Employee Bonuses (List & Hossain, 2009)

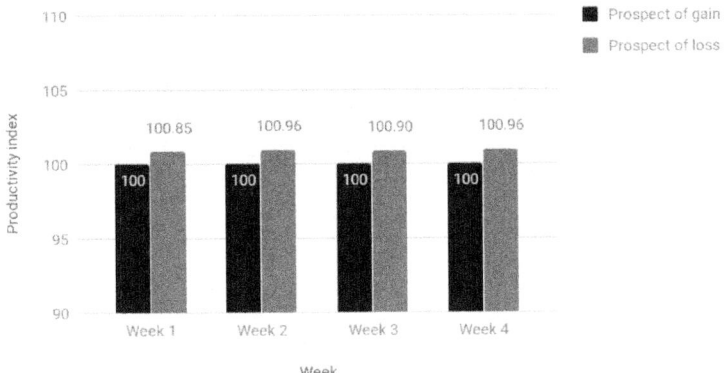

The group told that they had been provisionally awarded the bonus were consistently more productive (+1% p/week) than those told they would earn the bonus at the end of each week if they met a given production target. The difference was consistent over time. The results were not simply a consequence of workers misunderstanding of the system.

Again, the endowment effect was in play. Those provisionally awarded the bonus believed it was already theirs. They had been endowed with it. As a result, they valued the bonus more highly and were more productive in order to retain it.

Product Gems

1. **Create a sense of ownership**
   Allowing people to feel ownership of a product, even if they don't yet own it, is a powerful way for them to attribute value and an emotional connection to what you're offering.

2. **Embrace free trials or money-back guarantees**
   If you have a digital product, such as an app or a magazine subscription, you could experiment with offering a free trial for that product. This reduces the initial cost, and thus initial risk, of the decision-making process to zero. However, it also makes it less likely that when the free trial is over that the user will give up the product. The endowment effect means that they are going to feel some pain about surrendering the product. You can achieve the same effect with physical products by offering a generous money-back guarantee or returns policy, as both will endow the customer with your product.

3. **Seek commitment**
   The personalisation of a product early on in the ordering process, such as a free week-long test drive of that car you always wanted, or even a designer sketching a vision for how your new product experience could look. These ideas are just some examples of how you can engender a deep sense of pre-ownership and a strong, unwavering attachment and desire to buy as a result (see: IKEA effect).

4. **Build endowment into transaction drop-off points**
   If a customer adds something to their basket on an e-commerce store, but hasn't yet checked out, do think about sending them a polite reminder that the

product is "essentially theirs, but for a single, simple click", or that they're "almost there" (see: sunk cost fallacy). Similarly, emphasising the speed at which the product can be delivered (i.e., next-day delivery) or specifying the exact date creates a real connection with its arrival.

5. **Boost employee productivity**
As seen in the final experiment, endowing someone with a bonus at the start of the year is likely to make them work harder to ensure they receive it twelve months later. This goes against conventional thought where bonuses are traditionally calculated at the end-of-year.

6. **Beware of overvaluation**
The endowment effect explains why businesses are more likely to overvalue their assets, especially when they are traded infrequently (e.g., closing a store or factory and having to sell the property). Similarly, managers may be more reluctant to trade less productive and familiar assets for more productive and unfamiliar ones, creating an enormous opportunity cost. Take an IT department, they might be averse to switching to new and improved software product because they are endowed to, and thus overvalue, the status quo (see: sunk cost fallacy, status quo bias).

9. IKEA Effect

We place a disproportionately higher value on self-made products

Labour alone can be sufficient to induce greater liking for the fruits of one's labour. Even constructing a mundane task can lead people to overvalue their (often poorly constructed) creations.

I was finally able to put some of the woodworking skills I learned at school to good use recently. An old wooden table in my back garden was on its last legs, literally. After borrowing tools from friends and family, construction began.

What would take a carpenter a few hours took me a few weekends. Mistakes in cuts, ordering the wrong screws, and holes drilled in the wrong place resulted in very slow progress. Alas, I persevered.

Now that it's complete, we eat outside on it every night, even when it rains (which is most of the time here in the UK). Friends have afforded it great compliments. At one point, I was so impressed with the outcome I considered changing careers to build tables full-time. The truth is, the table is not that impressive when lined up against store-bought alternatives, though the table was a labour of love and now has a special place in our house.

As my experience suggests, it turns out we are willing to pay more (and not less) for something that we've put labour into than for something bought ready-made, and it doesn't just apply to physical products.

Betty Crocker

When instant cake mixes were introduced in the 1950s as part of a broader trend to simplify the life of the American housewife by minimising manual labour, housewives were initially resistant. The mixes made cooking too easy, making their labour and skill seem undervalued.

Learning this, Betty Crocker, one of the leading manufacturers of mixes, changed their recipe to require adding an egg. This simple change caused sales to skyrocket. Infusing the task with labour appeared to be a crucial ingredient in the product's success.

When people create products with their own labour, their effort increases their perception of the end product's valuation. And while some labour is enjoyable and allows for product customisation—both of which might increase valuation—research suggests that labour alone can be sufficient to induce greater liking and value associated with the results.

IKEA Boxes

Fifty participants were each paid $5 to take part in an experiment (Ariely et al., 2012). The participants were split into two groups.

One group of participants was asked to assemble a plain black IKEA 'Kassett' storage box (builders). These participants were given an unassembled box with the assembly instructions included with the product. The other group of participants were given a fully assembled box and were given the opportunity to inspect it (non-builders).

After the initial stage—either building or inspecting the box—the participants were asked to submit a bid for the box. If their bid was equal to or above that of a randomly drawn price, they would pay that amount and take the box home. However, if their bid was below the price, they would forfeit the opportunity to purchase the box.

After stating their willingness to pay, participants rated how much they liked the box on a 7-point scale from 1 (not at all) to 7 (very much).

IKEA Boxes (Ariely et al., 2012)

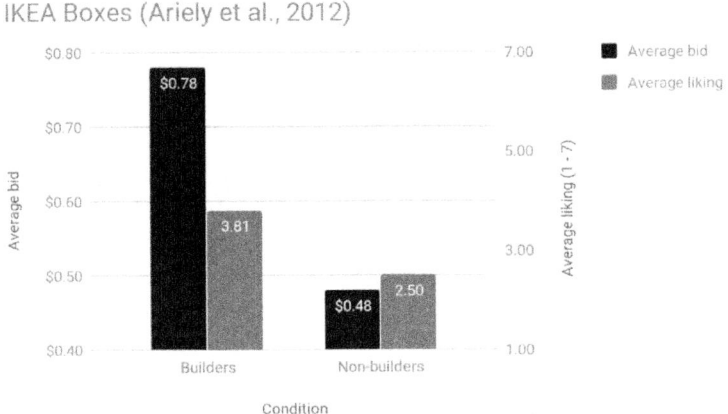

Not only did the builders bid significantly more for their boxes (M = $0.78) than non-builders (M = $0.48), they also reported greater liking for their box (M = 3.81) than the non-builders (M = 2.50).

While both groups were given a chance to buy the same product, those who assembled their own box valued it more than those who were given a chance to buy an identical pre-assembled box.

Origami

Having demonstrated that the IKEA effect occurs for mundane, practical products, researchers then changed the type of product.

In this experiment, 106 participants were split into three groups (Ariely et al., 2012). One group of participants were provided with an instruction sheet and a piece of high-quality origami paper and asked to make either an origami crane or an origami frog (builders). A second group were shown the completed origami figures created by the builder's group (non-builders, low-quality). The third group of participants were shown high-quality origami frogs and origami cranes created by origami experts (non-builders, high-quality).

After the initial stage—either building or inspecting the creations—participants were asked to submit a bid for the origami between $0.00 and $1.00. They were then told that if their bid was equal to or higher than a random price drawn by a researcher, they would pay that amount to purchase the creation. If their bid was below the number, they would go home empty-handed.

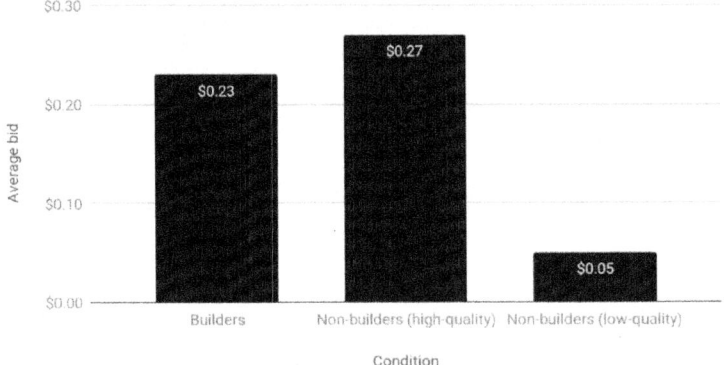

Origami (Ariely et al., 2012)

As expected, the builders' valuation of their origami was significantly higher (M = $0.23) than non-builders, and they were willing to pay for their low-quality creations (M = $0.05). Builders valued their origami so highly they were willing to pay nearly as much for their own creations as the non-builders were willing to pay for the high-quality origami made by the experts (M = $0.27).

While the non-builders saw the amateurish creations of the builders as nearly worthless crumpled paper, the builders valued their creations almost as much as the creations of experts.

LEGO

In their next experiment, researchers wanted to examine the role of task completion and the emergence of the IKEA effect.

In this experiment, 118 participants were paired up (59 pairs of participants) (Ariely et al., 2012). Each participant was given one of four LEGO sets, resembling a helicopter, a bird, a dog, or a duck when complete. Participants in each pair were always assigned different LEGO sets.

The pairs were split into three conditions. The first group of pairs were provided with a pre-assembled set (endowment), the second was given an unassembled LEGO kit and instructions to build it themselves (build), the third group of pairs were also given an unassembled LEGO kit, however, they were asked to disassemble the kit once they had completed building it (unbuild).

All participants were then instructed to place bids on both their own and their partner's set, and that the highest bidder for each would pay their own bid amount and take the set home. The bidding procedure required participants to take into account their own willingness to pay and their partner's bids—a kind of market price.

LEGO (Ariely et al., 2012)

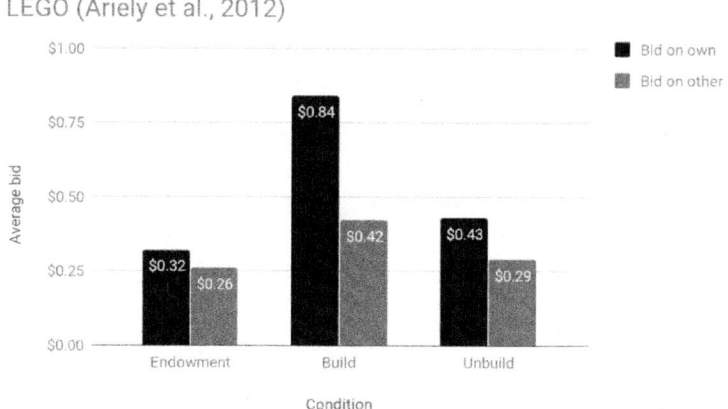

Participants valued their LEGO sets more when they built them (M = $0.84) compared to when they were endowed with pre-assembled sets (M = $0.32), and when they built and unbuilt their set (M = $0.43). Those who built their own sets valued them much more highly (M = $0.84) than their partner's creation (M = $0.42) too. The difference in bids between a participant's own creation and their partner's creation was less pronounced in the endowment (M = $0.32 vs. M = $0.26) and unbuild conditions (M = $0.43 vs. M = $0.29).

It was only in the build condition that participants' bids for their own creation were significantly higher than their bids for their partner's creations. When asked to build and destroy their creations, the valuations were closer to that of the endowment condition. This is particularly notable given that LEGO sets are designed to be assembled and taken apart, and participants could have quickly and easily reassembled their set had they bid enough to own it

We tend to place higher values on outcomes only when our labour and effort can be easily recognised.

Watches

Commercial research has also explored the IKEA effect. In one example, 165 participants agreed to take part in an experiment studying their willingness to pay for watches they could customise before purchase (Franke & Piller, 2004).

The researchers presented participants with a website allowing them to view two variations of a popular Swatch watch with different coloured wristbands. Participants were also asked to create their own customised version of the watch using an online configuration tool that allowed them to select from a limited number of component variations. As the configuration tool only allowed for limited customisations, participants were also asked to imagine their ideal version of the watch, where customisations were not limited by the choices available on the website.

Finally, participants were asked how much they are willing to pay for each of the standard watches, their custom creation, and their imaginary ideal watch.

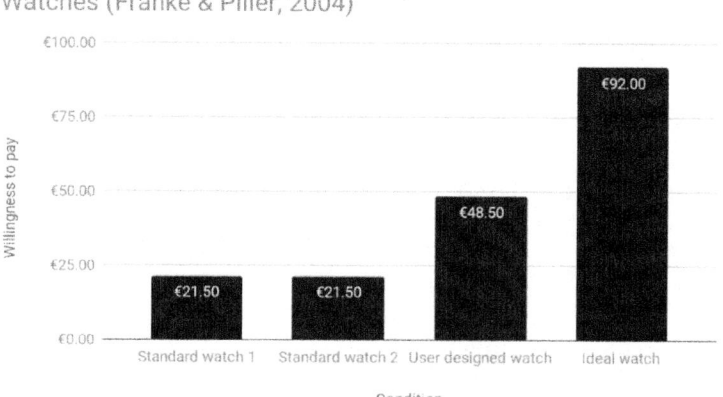

Watches (Franke & Piller, 2004)

Participants were willing to pay twice as much (M = €48.50) for their own limited self-designed watch than the actual cost of the two standard variations of the watch with the same technical quality (€21.50). When asked what price they would be willing to pay for their imaginary "ideal" watch, the average price jumped significantly (M = €92.00)

The experiment showed an enormous increase in a customer's willingness to pay for products they could customise before purchase.

Product Gems

1. **Give your prospects a choice**

   Look at how you can add in an aspect of customer-owned creation into your existing product or service. Even if the product is not physical, this is still possible. Getting the user to configure relevant features at the setup of software products can have the same effect. Similarly, in service-based products, giving the customer significant input when planning what work will be delivered can increase their perceived value of your offering.

2. **It's a value-add, not a labour-saving**

   Ensure that you market these changes as a value-added experience decision, not a labour-saving exercise. To some extent, the perception of this may depend on your brand. A good example of this is the Build-A-Bear product which allows people to make their own teddy bears. Many consumers enjoy this option, even though they are charged a high price for a product for which, thanks to their labour, the manufacturer does not have to pay production costs.

3. **Don't wait too long**

   Provide personalisation options early on in your user flow to create a sense of ownership and significantly reduce conversion drop-off later in the order process. Software products are particularly good at doing this by providing sample data, pre-filled defaults, and editable templates to help users customise the product from their very first engagement with it.

4. **Assign labour wisely**

   Where there are multiple stakeholders in a sales process, try to identify the decision maker or someone they trust, and get them to spend time with your product. Large organisations have a tendency to assign pre-work to those who don't have a say in the final decision. While those conducting the planning or setup will have a heightened sense of value for your product, the same effect will not be shared with the decision makers, as shown in the LEGO experiment.

5. **Beware of too much choice**

   The choice paradox tells us too much choice can be paralysing for consumers. Don't overload consumers with product choice assuming the additional labour and effort on their part will increase their perceived value.

6. **Don't fall victim to the effect**

   The IKEA effect is thought to contribute to the sunk cost fallacy, which frequently occurs in businesses when managers continue to devote resources to sometimes failing projects they have invested their labour in. The effect is also related to the "not invented here" syndrome, where managers disregard good ideas developed elsewhere, in favour of (possibly inferior) internally developed ideas.

10. Confirmation Bias

We seek out or interpret information in a way that confirms our preconceptions

When we have made a decision or build an opinion, we will actively seek things which will confirm them. We will also avoid things which will challenge them.

According to the flat Earth model of the universe, the sun and the moon are the same size. The earth does not orbit around them, as it does not orbit. Instead, the sun and moon move in rotating spheres some 2,500 miles above us.

The flat Earth model also finds the North Pole at the centre, and, at the outer limits, Antarctica. What most think of as the southernmost continent, is an ice wall wrapped around the earth's perimeter like a frame. Flat Earth believers contend that this ice wall "keeps the water in".

You'll find credible looking mathematical models that argue the theory, photographs taken from a plane showing a flat horizon, and queries about how the seas could ever exist if the earth was round. You won't find calculations from Eratosthenes who is credited for discovering the earth was round, photographs taken from space of a round planet, or the widely known force, gravity, which holds the water in the seas.

Anything that supports their claims is prominently cited and added to stoke the fire of their fervent belief, while evidence that goes against their hypotheses is often brushed aside or used to fuel new conspiracy theories.

Confirmation bias isn't limited to conspiracy theorists. It causes us to vote for politicians, investors to make poor decisions, businesses to focus on the wrong ideas, and almost certainly led you to buy this book.

Amazon Wish Lists

Think for a moment; what was the underlying reason you bought this book? Forget the well-crafted blurb or the cover art. Think about the decision you made when walking into the bookstore, or more likely, the words you entered into the Amazon.com search bar.

It is almost certain that you believe in the very predictable nature of human psychology and wanted to learn more. Those who don't share your beliefs are unlikely to ever find this book. Take a minute to consider your Amazon Wish List. Most people rarely seek books which challenge their notions of how things are or should be.

During the 2008 US presidential election, Valdis Krebs analysed purchasing trends on Amazon. People who already supported Obama were the same people buying books which painted him in a positive light. People who already disliked Obama were the ones buying books painting him in a negative light.

People weren't buying books for the information; they were buying them for the confirmation.

Numerical Sequences

One of the most popular ways of teaching the confirmation bias demonstrates that people are indeed biased towards confirming their existing beliefs and pragmatically assess the costs of being wrong.

Twenty-nine participants were told that the three numbers "2, 4, 6", conformed to a simple relational rule and that their task was to discover the rule by making up successive sets of three numbers (Wason, 1960).

For every three numbers the participants tried, the experimenter would tell them whether it satisfied the rule or not. For example, the participant might guess the next three numbers to be "8, 10, 12", and the researcher would confirm or deny if this sequence conformed to the rule.

There was no limit to the number combinations each participant was allowed to try until they felt sure about what the rule was and stopped to submit it to the researcher. However, they were explicitly told to discover the rule citing as few number combinations as possible.

Numerical Sequences (Wason, 1960)

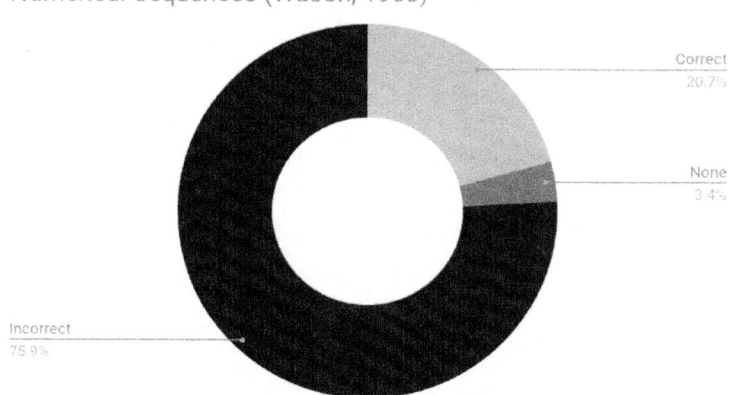

Correct
20.7%

None
3.4%

Incorrect
75.9%

The rule researchers used was that the numbers must be in ascending order. That is, any series of increasing numbers will conform to the rule. "1, 29, 30", "6, 7, 8", or "50, 100, 1000" would all fit the rule. However, a sequence like "10, 9, 8" would not.

Only 20.7% (six) of the participants actually submitted the correct rule. Some of the most common incorrect rules submitted were increasing intervals of two, multiples of the first number, and consecutive even numbers.

Almost all participants tried number combinations that proved the rule they finally submitted. Take those who believed the rule was increasing intervals of two. They tried sequences like "6, 8, 12", then "20, 22, 24" before submitting their rule. Very few actually tried to make up a number sequence that might disprove their hypothesis.

The participants formed a positive test strategy. Participants did not ask questions to falsify their hypothesis because as much as possible they did not want to break their own rules. Generally, people find this difficult to do, for they do not want to face the possibility that their beliefs could be wrong.

Job Suitability (part 1)

The past heavily influences both our current and future beliefs. Another group of researchers wanted to understand how our confirmation bias can affect the way we remember things when making decisions.

Thirty-three participants were asked to read 4.5 pages about a week in the life of an imaginary woman named Jane (Snyder, 1979). Jane did things that showed she could be extroverted in some situations (e.g., socialising during her coffee break) and introverted in a similar number of other situations (e.g., remained shy and timid at the supermarket).

Two days later, the participants returned. Researchers divided the participants into two groups and asked them to help decide if Jane would be suited for a particular job.

One group was asked if she would be suited to a job as a research librarian and explicitly told the best research librarians had introverted traits. The other group was asked if she would be suited to a job as a real estate salesperson and explicitly told the best real estate salespeople had extroverted traits.

Participants were then asked to write down all of Jane's personal traits from the story that they considered relevant to assessing how well-suited Jane was for the job in question.

Job Suitability (part 1) (Snyder, 1979)

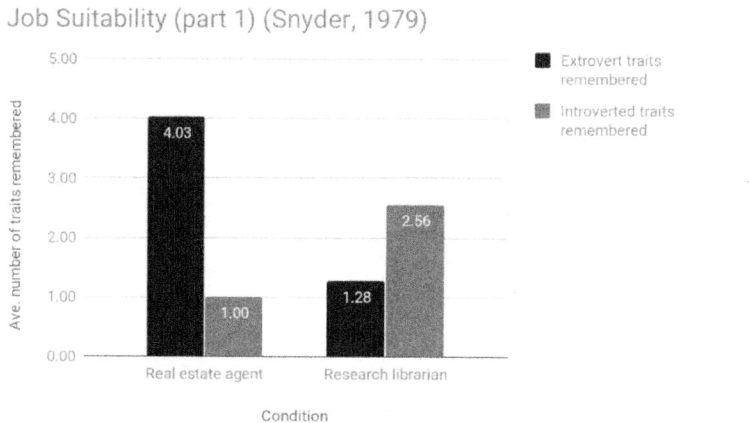

Researchers found that the participants considering Jane for the position of real estate salesperson (extroverted job type) saw her more as an extrovert, remembering more of her extroverted traits (M = 4.03) than introverted ones (M = 1.00). However, participants considering Jane for a research librarian position (introverted job type) saw her as an introvert, remembering almost twice as many of her introverted traits (M = 2.56) than extroverted ones (M = 1.28).

Participants' recall was heavily influenced by information they learned about each job.

Job Suitability (part 2)

Continuing the same experiment, researchers then asked all participants, half whom believed Jane was an introvert and the other half an extrovert, to report their judgments of her suitability for the job of real estate salesperson and research librarian on a 6-point scale from 1 (extremely unsuited) to 6 (extremely well suited) (Snyder, 1979).

Job Suitability (part 2) (Snyder, 1979)

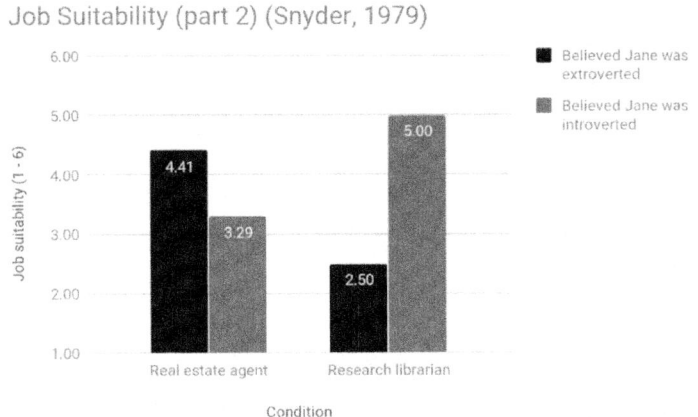

Those that reported Jane to have more extroverted traits believed she would make an above average real estate salesperson (M = 4.41), a job well suited to extroverts, but a below average research librarian (M = 2.50), a job more suited to introverts. In doing so, they were confirming their belief Jane was an extrovert. Similarly, those that reported Jane to have more introverted believed the opposite. While they reported here a being well suited as a research librarian (M = 5.00) they believed she would make a much worse real estate salesperson (M = 3.29)

The study suggests our memories fall prey to confirmation bias, recalling those things that support even recently arrived at beliefs and forgetting those things that contradict them.

Hiring

The job suitability experiment has real implications for the way hiring managers make decisions. In many cases, bad ones. The researchers were able to clearly demonstrate this in action using another experiment.

This time, twenty-five new participants were asked to prepare two lists of the traits that they would want to know about a candidate applying for the position of research librarian and for a real estate salesperson (Snyder, 1979). In essence, they were crafting two job descriptions. Participants were then asked to rate if the traits they listed made someone "suited" or "unsuited" to the job. For example, they might want to know if the real estate salesperson candidate could drive (suited) or had no experience selling homes (unsuited).

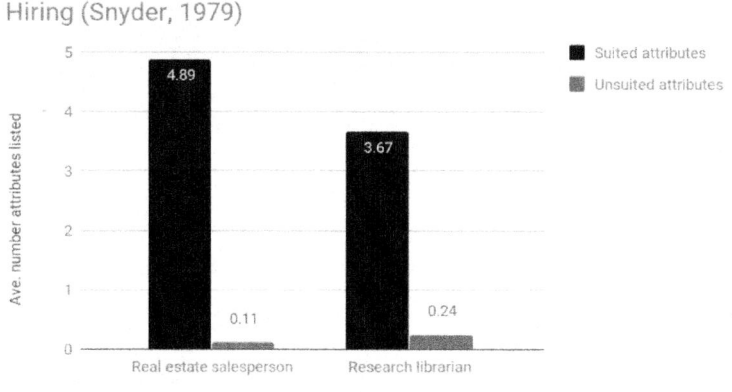

Hiring (Snyder, 1979)

The participants wrote down significantly more suited attributes (4.89 for real estate salesperson / 3.67 for research librarian) than unsuited attributes (0.11 for real estate salesperson / 0.24 for research librarian)

Again, the participants were using a positive test strategy to craft what they believed to be a perfect candidate.

The same set of researchers also examined 7415 "Help wanted" ads in local newspapers alongside this study. They found only 33 ads informed prospective candidates of attributes that would make them unsuited for the job being advertised, while the remaining 7382 contained only attributes that would make candidates suitable for the job in question.

The confirmation bias can result in neglect of key pieces of information that are inconsistent with our own beliefs.

Political Views (part 1)

The confirmation bias is perhaps most apparent in supporters of opposing political parties and is the reason why many voters support the same party for their entire lives.

In one experiment, 156 participants were asked to respond to seventeen questions about different political issues (Knobloch-Westerwick et al., 2009). Issues included gun ownership and abortion. The participants rated their support for each issue on an 11-point scale from -5 (strongly opposing) to 5 (strongly supporting).

Six weeks later, participants returned and were asked to browse an online news magazine. Four political issues chosen from the seventeen original issues were covered in eight articles, with half the articles featuring opposing beliefs to those of the participant and the other half of articles containing content that supported the participants' political beliefs.

Political Views (part 1) (Knobloch-Westerwick et al., 2009)

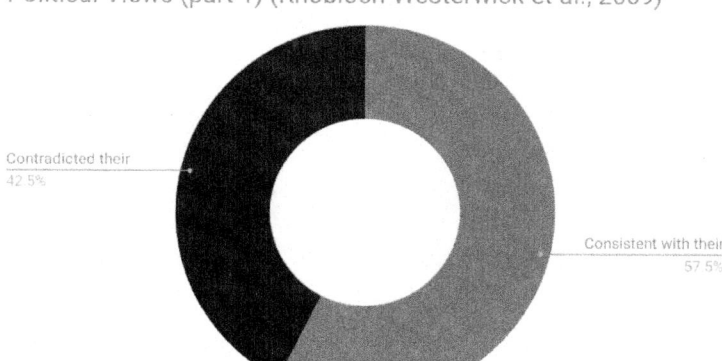

Contradicted their
42.5%

Consistent with their
57.5%

The participants were much more likely to choose an article with a message confirming their beliefs (57.5%) versus one that contradicted them (42.5%).

The participants actively sought media that supported their views, or put another way, didn't challenge their beliefs.

Interestingly, in another experiment examining how people processed the political satire of a predominantly left-wing US comedy talk-show, The Colbert Report, researchers found audiences interpreted the content in a manner that best fit with their individual political beliefs, both right and left wing (LaMarre et al., 2009).

Political Views (part 2)

As part of the same experiment, the researchers also monitored how long the participants spent reading articles that supported and opposed their views on the political issue raised (Knobloch-Westerwick et al., 2009).

Political Views (part 2) (Knobloch-Westerwick et al., 2009)

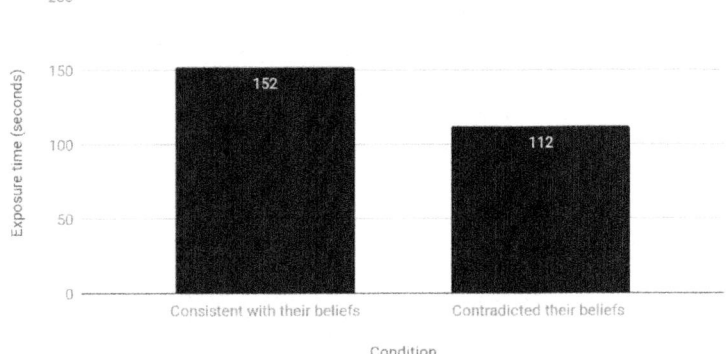

Participants spent 152 seconds on average looking at articles consistent with their beliefs, and only 112 seconds on opposing articles. Put another way, the participants spent 40 more seconds (36%) on articles that confirmed their attitudes than those that challenged them!

We are much more likely to select and spend time on material that aligns with our current beliefs when compared with information that opposes our beliefs.

Product Gems

1. **Stay open-minded**
   When there are disagreements, conduct a non-emotional discussion or debate with those who offer up opposing views and see how they came up with their belief. This can be especially useful in prospect- or customer-focused meetings. Sharing experiences and reasoning might open one party's mind to the others way of thinking.

2. **Be careful with your research**
   Product designers should be careful when researching new features. Make sure any research covers a diverse set of participants. Set yourself a goal to invalidate your hypotheses and recognise when your ego is influencing your work.

3. **Push teams to prove assumptions wrong**
   Warren Buffett, one of the most successful investors of our time, is well aware of confirmation bias and one of his first actions before making an investment decision is to seek opinions that contradict his own. At one annual investor meeting, Buffett invited hedge fund trader Doug Kass to participate. Kass is a critic of Buffett and his investment style.

4. **Prototype and test aggressively (and plan for refinement)**
   When we understand that our first assumptions will not be correct and plan for failure, we allow teams to find the correct answer instead of going with a simple and easy hypothesis.

5. **Ask better questions**
   One of the most worthless questions to ask a customer is "How did we do?" It's worthless because you'll never get any constructive feedback.

A much better question is "What could we have done differently to make it better?" By changing the question ever so slightly, you'll be shocked at the honest advice you'll hear.

6. **Think about market biases**

   Consider how the market views some of your messaging, especially for highly innovative products. You might hear people talk about products that were "too early for the market". If there are existing confirmation biases in your target customer base, it can be an expensive and time-consuming task to get consumer eyeballs if you're introducing a proposition that tests their existing beliefs. This is especially true if you are shaping a sales strategy to steal customers from a market incumbent who has told them for years "how it should be done" (see: status quo bias).

7. **Data helps, but be careful**

   Qualitative measures are much better to use in arguments due to their inherent factual nature. However, you should make it clear how data points should be interpreted. A 2013 study found that confirmation bias can affect the way that people view statistics (Kahan, 2013). Its authors report that people have a tendency to infer information from statistics that support their existing beliefs, even when the data supports an opposing view.

8. **Surround yourself with a diverse group of people**

   Try to build a diverse team of individuals. Don't hire because you think you've got an idea of the perfect candidate. Discuss your thoughts with your existing team and don't be afraid to foster to dissenting views. Seek out people that challenge your opinions, perhaps someone in a different team, or assign someone on your team to play "devil's advocate" for major decisions.

11. Present Bias

What we want now is not what we aspire to in the future

We give stronger weight to payoffs that are closer to the present moment when considering future moments. The closer to the present moment, the less rational we become (though only up to a point!).

Future bias would yield quotations you seldom hear; I plan to eat more cookies and doughnuts next year, I plan to borrow more on my credit card next year, I plan to exercise less next year, or I plan to wake up later next year.

New Year resolutions, a popular tradition in many countries, highlight our focus on the present. For some they are effective (see: fresh start effect). However, more often than not a few weeks into the year and our good intentions have weakened. The healthy options are shunned, takeaways are charged to the credit card, and the gym membership has long been forgotten.

This behaviour is symptomatic of what is known as present bias. Present bias is the tendency to over-value immediate rewards at the expense of our long-term intentions – a trait that can have big implications later on.

As aspirational creatures, our intentions are generally good. We all want to spend less, save more. We want to choose products that we should consume, as opposed to wanting to consume. The problem is; time has a curious effect on the quality of our decisions.

Research has shown that we make drastically different choices for the near-future compared to those made for the more distant future.

$1 or $3?

There is a well-known scenario that exposes our present bias. People are asked the questions: "Would you prefer a dollar today or three dollars tomorrow?" or "Would you prefer a dollar in one year or three dollars in one year and one day?".

Most findings show a significant fraction of those questioned have no problem choosing the higher figure for the distant future but find it hard to be patient when the smaller amount is right in front of them. Individuals with such preferences are described as "present-biased".

Think of it another way; if you were asked in twelve months time whether you would work an extra seven-hour day on April 1st or an extra eight hours on April 30th, most would choose the seven hours on April 1st.

However, if next year on March 30th, we were asked the same question, we would be more likely to choose the eight hours on April 30th. The thought of working seven hours the next day is enough to put it off for four weeks. This is time-inconsistent behaviour -- we choose differently depending on how close in the future the outcome is.

Present bias is related to the thinking trap known as hyperbolic discounting. Given two similar rewards, humans show a preference for one that arrives sooner rather than later. Humans are said to discount the value of the later reward, by a factor that increases with the length of the delay.

The present bias occurs when individuals place a greater value on goods or income achieved in the present moment

– rather than receiving the same goods or income in the future.

Given a choice between a payoff today and a payoff in the future; we typically choose to have the payoff now. For example, a firm sending out invoices would generally prefer the money upfront, rather than the riskier option of getting paid in addition of interest in the future.

Pension Pots

The UK has the lowest state pension of any developed country. The average private sector retiree is likely to receive just 29% of their previous earnings from their public pension, with many relying on private pensions. As a result, in the early 2000s, the UK government realised it needed to act with worryingly low pension saving rates among private sector workers.

In order to increase pensions savings, the Government mandated employers to establish an "automatic enrolment" pension scheme in 2012 (UK Office for National Statistics, 2016). This meant that workers would be automatically placed into a company's pension scheme, and contributions would be deducted from their pay packet unless they formally requested to be exempted.

The theory was that many people actually wanted to put more money aside for retirement, but they were "presently-biased" and therefore put-off from doing so by the need to make what they feared would be complicated decisions.

The idea was that auto-enrolment would make saving the default for employees, and thus make it easier for them, or nudge them, to do what they really wanted to do and increase the amount they were contributing to a pension.

Pension Pots (UK Office of National Statistics, 2016)

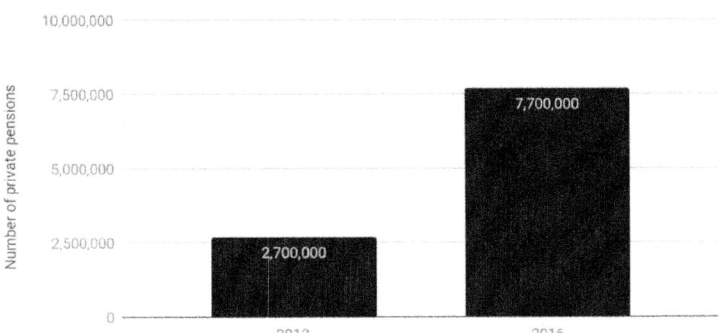

Since auto-enrolment was introduced by the Government in 2012, active membership of private sector pension schemes has jumped from 2.7 million to 7.7 million in 2016.

Behavioural nudges are alternatives to using standard government interventions in markets (e.g. through taxes and subsidies) to influence the choices that people make in their everyday lives. Governments can use them effectively to counteract the present bias in the population to increase citizens wellbeing and prosperity.

Sunscreen

The first week of spring in England is synonymous with bulbs flowering in a beautiful array of colours, and peoples skin turning to a darker shade of red as it is exposed to the sun for the first time in 6 months. Many know sunscreen will lower our risk of skin cancer, however, find the fact hard to quantify because the damaging effects of the sun are only really visible much later in life.

Researchers looking into the use of sunscreen believed framing health-related messages could reduce present bias in the population, and in-turn increase consumption of sunscreen to protect from the damaging effects of the sun.

On a sunny day, researches headed to the coast to question beachgoers (Detweiler et al., 1999) -- my kind of experiment! First, participants were asked to fill out a questionnaire to determine if they intended to use sunscreen during their trip (their tendency for present bias).

Once the two groups of participants had been classified as having or not having a previous intention to use sunscreen, researchers then showed half of the participants in each group a brochure with one of two messages about skin cancer:

1. Framed potential gains: "Protect yourself from the sun and you will stay healthy".
2. Framed potential losses: "Expose yourself to the sun and you will risk becoming sick".

After reading the brochures, all participants were given a coupon for a free sample of sunscreen and were told they could redeem it 30 minutes later.

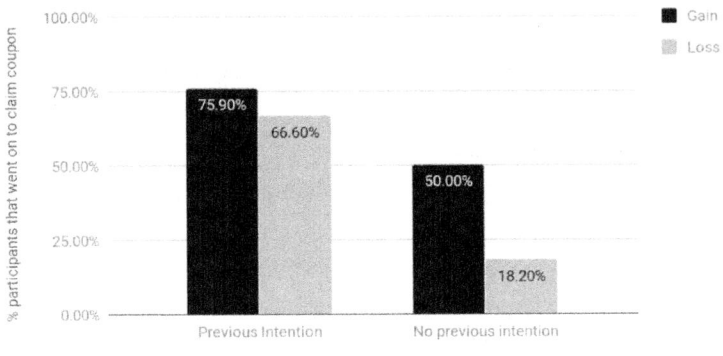

Sunscreen (Detweiler et al., 1999)

As expected, those with previous intentions to use sunscreen during their visit to the beach were much likely to redeem their coupon for a free bottle of sunscreen (M = 71.25%) than those who had no previous intention to use sunscreen during their visit (M = 39.1%).

Those who showed a present bias, that is those who were not planning on using sunscreen before reading the brochure, reacted very differently to the loss and gain variation messages. When presented with a loss, participants were less likely to redeem their coupon for free sunscreen (M = 18.2%) compared to those who read the gains they could achieve through using sunscreen (M = 50.0%) -- a figure much closer to the redemption levels seen in the participants already intending to use sunscreen.

Prospect theory suggests that people respond differently to factually equivalent messages depending on how these messages are framed (Tversky & Kahneman, 1981). Present bias can be mitigated by framing outcomes.

Grocery Shopping (part 1)

Health outcomes are, generally, quite distant -- we don't expect to be diagnosed with cancer tomorrow. Even with the positive effects framing can produce, health organisations often struggle to convey educational messages to populations for this reason (see: availability heuristic). Over shorter periods of time, self-control can prove more difficult to combat (Schelling, 1984), especially when it comes to food.

Hyperbolic discounting causes us to devalue future outcomes in favour of the now. Researchers also argued not only would people discount future outcomes in-line with the hyperbolic discounting theory, but that their preferences would also distinctly differ when they made choices for the near term when compared to the more distant future.

Researchers analysed online transactions conducted by customers who ordered groceries from a leading U.S. retailer between January 1, 2005, and December 31, 2005 (Milkman et al., 2008). The online retailer offered varying lead times from placing an order to its delivery -- for some orders, this was up-to five days.

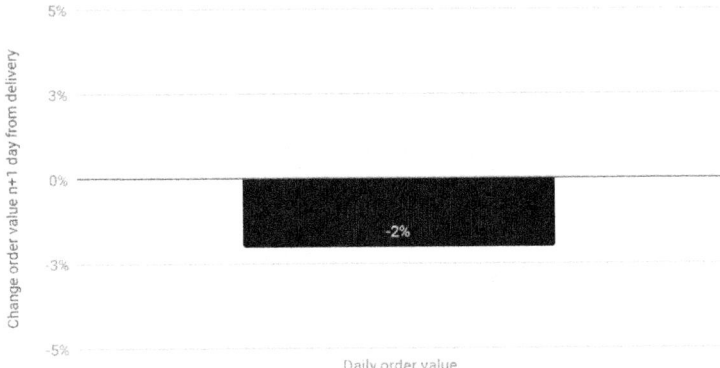

Grocery Shopping (part 1) (Milkman et al., 2008)

Analysing the data set, the researchers found the dollar size of a grocery order decreased by approximately 2% for each additional day that separated a customer's last visit to the online retailers' website and the date when their groceries were delivered.

Customers spend more money the faster they can receive an item. We behave more impulsively and struggle to a greater extent with self-control the sooner our decisions will take effect -- as many fellow Amazon Prime will attest.

Grocery Shopping (part 2)

Researchers wanted to look at how the makeup of a customer's orders changed when compared to the delivery date. The first analysis showed customers were spending more when they could receive their groceries more quickly; but how did the type of groceries in the order differ based on delivery date?

To examine this, researchers classified the 117 categories of food offered by the online retailer (e.g. Frozen Vegetables, Cream, Cookies, etc.) on a 7-point scale from 1 ("want") to 7 ("should").

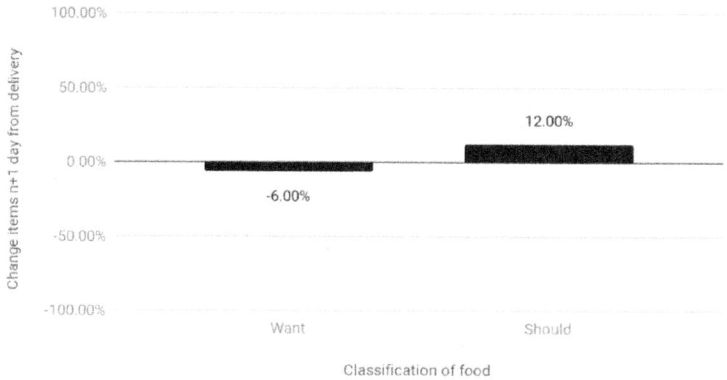

Grocery Shopping (part 2) (Milkman et al., 2008)

When examining the items in each customer's order, researchers uncovered that they contained healthier, should items, the longer the lead time was for delivery. With each day the delivery date increased, the number of healthy groceries in the basket increased by 12% whilst unhealthy, want items, decreased by 6%.

Customer impulse was driven mainly by unhealthy, want decisions. Shoppers have a stronger preference for should goods and a weaker preference for want goods the further in advance of consumption they make their selections. As aspirational creatures, our intentions are generally good.

University Essays

Procrastination is all too familiar to most people, myself included. Writing a book provides ample time for procrastination -- tidying the house, sorting out bills, or replying to old emails.

Though we've explored the effect time, specifically time-discounting, has on our decisions. Many of us are acutely aware we're time-inconsistent and tend to make suboptimal choices in the present. Two researchers explored this idea using students enrolled in an executive-education course at MIT (Ariely & Wertenbroch, 2002).

Three short papers were required to complete the course. Each paper had a deadline, with a 1% grade penalty per day late for all subjects. The students on the course were split into two groups:

1. No-choice: Were given evenly spaced deadlines by their lecturers.
2. Free-choice: Each student free to impose their own deadlines (or not).

In the free-choice group, 37 out of 51 students imposed deadlines on themselves in an attempt to mitigate time penalties, or put another way, overcome their present bias. The average deadline they set themselves for paper 1 was 42 days before the end of the term, for paper 2 it was about 26 days before the end of the term, and for paper 3 was about 10 days before the end of the term.

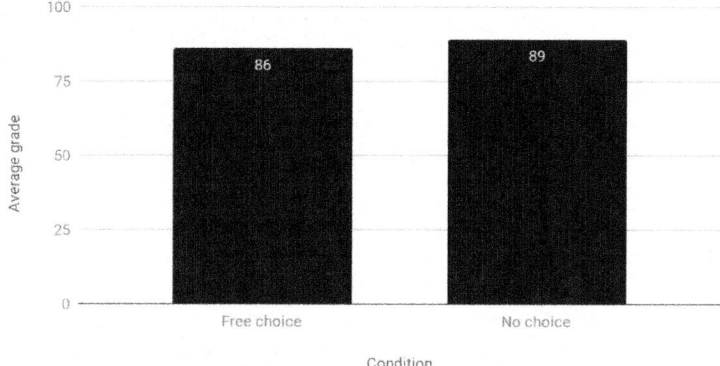

University Essays (Ariely & Wertenbroch, 2002)

Despite the free-choicers having the flexibility to set deadlines, average grades in the no-choice group were higher, with an average grade of 89 versus 86.

In a rational world, where self-control was not an issue, participants would not have set a deadline. However the students were well aware they were prone to procrastination. People in the free-choice chose to make costly commitments upfront, which is consistent with present bias and some degree of sophistication. However, the chosen commitments were far from optimal, suggesting naivete, and as such, they performed worse than the no-choice students.

We know we're time-inconsistent but find it incredibly difficult to predict how to most optimally balance our self-control in the future.

Product Gems

1. **Understand the power of time**
   We weigh present rewards more heavily than future ones. Given a choice between a payoff today and a payoff in the future; we typically choose to have the payoff now. Amazon Prime is a good example of this effect. Consumers are generally willing to pay more (or are less price sensitive to competition) when they can have the product in their hands tomorrow versus five days later. If you have a long delivery lead time, considerer giving customers a second opportunity to add to their order.

2. **Consumers lack self-control**
   If we are offered an instant reward, the incentive has to be very high for us to postpone the fulfilment. Case in point: the exorbitant interest rates banks charge on credit-card debt and other short-term personal loans, both of which exploit our emotional must-have-now instincts. Similarly, a tasty looking chocolate bar at the checkout of a supermarket can easily find its way into a customer's basket…

3. **Nudge healthy (or unhealthy) choices**
   Retailers could encourage shoppers to order their groceries up to 5 days in advance of delivery. This will lead to healthier choices. This is also known as "future lock-in" and can be used for all types of 'should' decisions beyond groceries that will end up benefiting the consumer. On the flip-side, given that customers are found to spend more and make more 'should' decisions as the time to delivery decreases, retailers could adapt the product recommendations to fit, offering naughty treats on severely-time-restricted special offer.

4. **Improve demand forecasting**
   Retailers can improve their demand forecasting by taking into account the fact that their customers may be likely to spend more in the near future than in the more distant future.
5. **Reduce the effects using commitments**
   Present bias can lead us to delay decisions. If you're attempting to change a consumer's behaviour, consider implementing commitments. For example, a travel agent could offer a "Buy now pay later" agreement whereby a certain percentage of a customer's salary is automatically debited from their account each week for a summer vacation (see: endowment effect).
6. **Understand consumers aspirations**
   One study used a novel way to get people to understand the importance of saving for retirement by making their "future self" more realistic to them now. Those who saw an image of themselves in the future consistently chose to put more of their savings aside. Marketers can take advantage of "the future" to reduce the effects of present bias.
7. **A powerful alternative for policymakers**
   Behavioural nudges can offer alternatives to using standard government interventions in markets (e.g. through taxes and subsidies) to influence the choices that people make in their everyday lives. From public health to the economy, nudges are proving an ever-popular way for governments to implement submissive measures to improve the lives of their populations. *Example: The UK Government's Behavioural Insights Team.*

12. Optimism Bias

When looking to our future, we tend to overestimate the good stuff and underestimate the bad

Our tendency to be too hopeful leads us to consistently overstate the expected success of our investments, the chances of achieving our future dreams, or even our perceived ability to avoid a car accident whilst driving drunk when compared to our friends.

Marriage. It's a wonderful thing, isn't it?

In the Western world, the numbers don't agree. Divorce rates are about 40 percent. That means that out of five married couples, two will end up in divorce. But when you ask newlyweds about their own likelihood of divorce, they estimate it at zero percent.

We not only underrate our chances of getting divorced, being in a car accident, or suffering from cancer, but we also expect to live longer than the average person, overestimate our success in the job market, and believe that our children will be especially talented.

We're optimistic about ourselves, we're optimistic about our kids, we're optimistic about our families, but we're not so optimistic about the guy sitting next to us, and we're somewhat pessimistic about the fate of our fellow citizens and the fate of our country.

Our private optimism about our own personal future doesn't mean that we think things will magically turn out okay, but rather that we have the unique ability to make it so. However, overly positive assumptions can lead to disastrous miscalculations.

New Restaurants

Do you ever find yourself in situations wondering "how hard could it be?".

As an amateur home-chef, I have a particularly bad habit of asking this type of question when dining out. How hard could it be to create a menu, cook the food, and delight the customers?

In some cities, the chance of restaurant failure in the first year can be as high as 90%. That is, nine out of every ten restaurants opened will fail. Restaurateurs know the numbers, but despite the well-documented failure rates, they often don't think they apply to them. They might argue their concept is different to the others, their restaurant is in a better part of town, or the cuisine is seeing new popularity.

Their optimism is a good thing. A society without this entrepreneurial optimism would lead to a limited range of choice. But do they really have a better chance of success than others trying the same thing? In 90% of cases, no. The dangers of being overly optimistic or self-confident can often blind us to the very high likelihood of negative outcomes.

Life Events (part 1)

There have been a number of experiments conducted around the world to explore the extent of our inherent optimism bias. In one well-known experiment, 120 participants were asked to make comparative judgments about the likelihood that specific events would happen to them (Weinstein, 1980). All participants were students at the same university.

Each participant was shown eighteen positive events (i.e., owning your own home) and twenty-four negative events (i.e., heart attack before age forty). They were then asked:

"Compared to other students—same sex as you at the same University—what do you think are the chances that the following events will happen to you?"

To report their answers, participants were given a range of choices in 20% increments from -100% less (no chance) to +100% more (definite chance).

Life Events (part 1) (Weinstein, 1980)

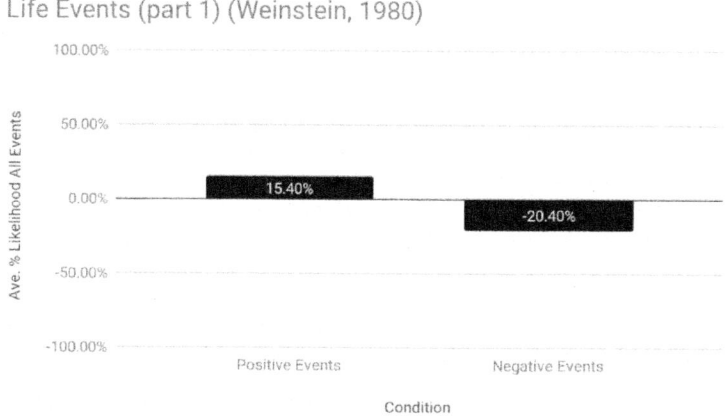

The results are clear. The participants believed they were much more likely to experience the positive events (M = 15.40%) over their fellow students. When considering the negative events, the participants believed they were much less likely to experience them compared to the other students (M = -20.40%).

We tend to have an unrealistic optimism for both positive and negative life events.

Life Events (part 2)

In many circumstances in the modern world, we compare ourselves to our peers. The researchers in the first experiment suggested that people may be optimistically biased because their image of other people is inaccurate or incomplete—we know more about ourselves than we ever could about someone else.

To examine this, seventy-eight participants of the same university took part in an experiment (Price et al., 2002). Each participant was shown twenty different negative life experiences (i.e., having a limb amputated).

All participants were first asked to estimate how often Americans experience each of the twenty negative life events. They rated the frequency of each event on a 9-point scale from 1 (extremely infrequent) to 9 (extremely frequent).

The participants were then split into two groups. One group was asked to compare their own chances of each event happening to them compared to other students at the university who were the same age and sex as themselves (self-risk). The second group was asked to state the chance the average student at their institution would experience each event (peer risk).

Each group was asked to rate the likelihood of events for each question on a scale from 1 (extremely low) to 7 (extremely high).

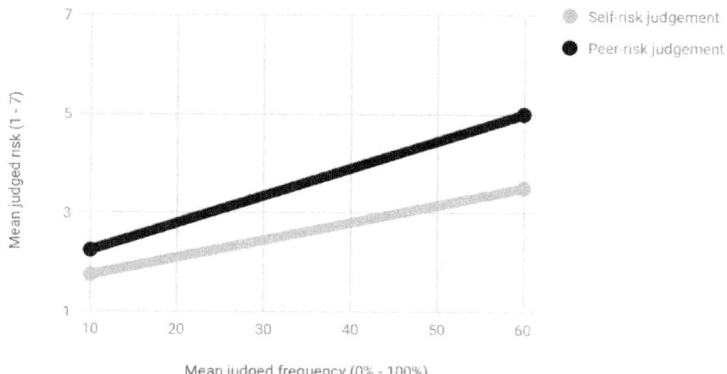

Life events (part 2) (Price et al., 2002)

Self-risk judgement

Peer-risk judgement

Mean judged risk (1 - 7)

Mean judged frequency (0% - 100%)

Participants believed they were much less likely to experience the negative events compared to similar students of the same university. **When asked to explicitly compare ourselves to similar peers, we have an unrealistic optimism for avoiding negative life events.**

The researchers also found participants rated both their own and their peers' risk of suffering more frequent negative events higher than infrequent ones. When an event was judged to occur frequently (60%), the participants assessed their own likelihood of suffering the event to be much lower (M = 3.50) than their peers (M = 5.00). However, for negative events judged to occur infrequently (10%), the participants perceived likelihood of suffering the event was only slightly lower (M = 1.75) than the likelihood they estimated for their peers (M = 2.25).

The more frequently we judge a negative event to occur, the greater the sense of optimism we have for ourselves over our peers (see: category size bias).

Life Events (part 3)

As humans, we can be stubborn. Beliefs and habits can often be hard to change. Another group of researchers wanted to test how our optimism changes when provided with contradictory evidence.

Nineteen participants were asked to estimate their odds of experiencing eighty unfavourable events, such as contracting various diseases or being the victim of a crime (Sharot, 2011).

After writing down their estimations, participants were then told the actual average probability of suffering these unfavourable events. Once they had finished learning the actual odds, they were asked to repeat the experiment and again estimate their odds of experiencing eighty unfavourable events.

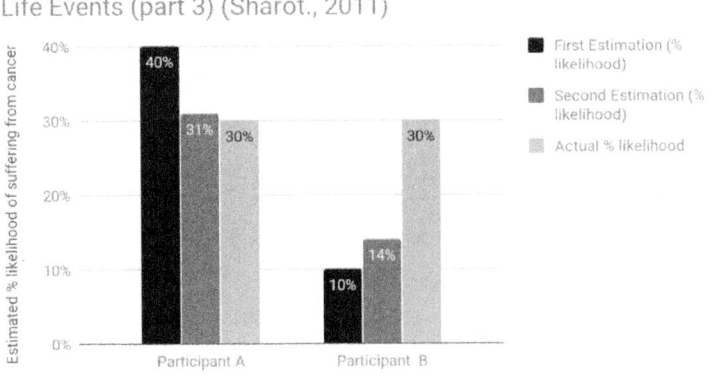

Life Events (part 3) (Sharot., 2011)

Participants' initial estimations varied significantly for each one of the unfavourable events. When two participants were asked estimated their odds of suffering from cancer, Participant A ranked their likelihood of getting cancer much higher (40%) than Participant B (10%). When both these participants were told the actual odds of getting cancer (30%), their second estimations showed an interesting change. Participant A who originally ranked their likelihood of getting cancer as much higher than the actual odds significantly reduced their estimation closer to the actual figure (31%). On the other hand, Participant B who believed their risk of getting cancer was significantly lower than the actual only slightly increased their estimate when asked again (14%).

Similar results were seen across all participants who took part in the experiment. Participants who received information that turned out to be more positive than their initial thoughts (i.e., a smaller chance of suffering from disease than expected), were more likely to reduce their new estimate to closely match the information they had been given. Those who received information worse than their original estimate tended not to change their estimations much.

People changed their beliefs selectively in light of only positive information, indicating that we're biased towards believing only the positive.

Online Privacy

The first three experiments considered almost identical scenarios. A group of researchers in Asia set up an experiment using a different scenario; testing optimism in relation to online privacy.

A total of 910 participants were split into two groups and each asked two questions about online privacy (Cho et al., 2010). The first group was asked:

1. How likely are you to become the victim of an invasion of online privacy?
2. How likely is it that your personal information will be stolen over the Internet?

The second group was asked a similar question; however, the word you/yours was replaced by others. The word "others" was explained to the participants as meaning "other people who are about your age and have similar social positions or jobs".

The two groups were then asked to answer both questions using a 7-point scale from 1 (very unlikely) to 7 (very likely).

Online privacy (Cho et al., 2010)

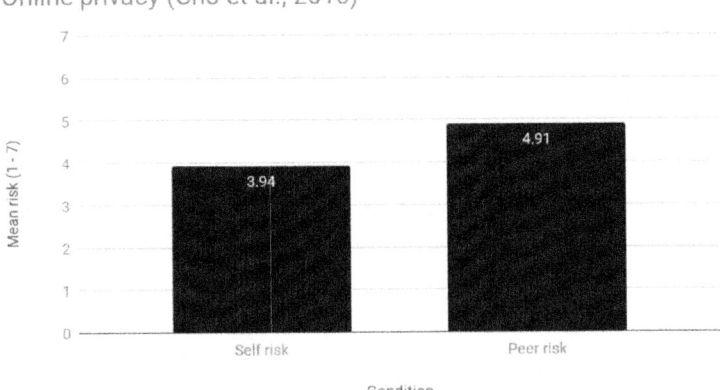

Overall, the respondents were quite confident about their ability to control their own risks associated with online privacy (M = 3.94) than their peers were (M = 4.91).

In line with previous experiments, the results show that the optimism bias can occur in almost all scenarios where a decision must be made with limited information available.

Product Gems

1. **Plan Carefully**
   Although our optimism bias will often cause us to overstate our likelihood of future success, it does not mean we should lower our goals. Think carefully about what you need to reach a goal you've set and put in place a plan to achieve it. Governments suffer from over-optimism so consistently that there are even detailed documents outlining how public servants should factor the bias into the planning of large projects.

2. **Account for consumer optimism**
   Your consumers' positive view of the future will need to be managed, especially for subscription-based products. It is likely that consumers will expect product improvements over time and risk being dissatisfied if these expectations are not delivered. For many companies, this might involve sharing parts of their product roadmap with prospects and customers. Essentially, it is about giving them as much information as possible to set their initial expectations accordingly.

3. **Use positive information motivate**
   Instead of telling people why they shouldn't do something, convince them with the benefits of an alternative. For example, telling people to stop smoking because it causes cancer is unlikely to stop someone smoking—remember our optimism bias leads us to think we're less likely to suffer negative outcomes compared to others. Offering a positive outcome to stop smoking (and reduce cancer), such as e-cigarettes, is much more likely to change a person's behaviour. Speak about the

benefits of your product, not the negatives of your competition.

4. **Make impending negative events caused by over-optimism clear**
Bringing negative events to our mind just before we're likely to engage in an undesirable act can be a good behaviour change technique. Germany's "piss screens" are a great example of this suggestion. To help reduce drink-driving, TV screens were placed above urinals showing a racing car video game that was controlled by the urinal. The drunker a person was, the slower the car on the screen travelled. If the person is too drunk, the game ends with a crash, prompting them to take a taxi home instead. The aim here is to make the negative effects of a certain action clear to the individual and offer a clear, positive alternative.

5. **Beware of sales optimism**
Sales managers take note! It's important to negate the potential costs of the optimism bias when estimating the expected time to complete a deal. We humans are notoriously bad at sticking to these estimates as we always tend to think it'll take a lot less time than it actually does. As a sales manager, remember to coach your team to factor in a proportional optimism bias multiplier into their estimations.

6. **Use other biases to limit the effects**
This bias is particularly important for decision makers creating health or safety products, where the dangers of being overly optimistic can lead to dreadful outcomes. Hospitals, nuclear power plants and oil refineries are good examples. There are two

researched ways of reducing the optimism bias; highlight the availability heuristic (make past bad events more easily retrievable from one's memory) and use loss aversion (highlight losses that are likely to occur because of these bad events) (Jolls & Sunstein, 2006). Incorporating these two concepts into product design or marketing collateral can go a long way towards helping reduce the risks of this bias.

7. **The effect isn't totally uniform across everyone**
   Though it's commonplace across gender, age and culture, rather aptly, the optimism bias doesn't seem to kick in for people suffering from depression—in fact, some argue they suffer a pessimism bias. This is worth remembering if you're designing solutions for such individuals. Interestingly, because of the absence of unrealistic levels of optimism, those with mild depression are actually much more accurate at predicting future events, seeing the world 'as it is', rather than perhaps how we'd like it to be.

13. Hedonic Adaptation

Restricting our pleasure increases our overall experience

A consumer's enjoyment of a product or service can be enhanced by interruptions, breaks, or limitations. What we want isn't always what makes us happiest. Without restrictions, we find it difficult to moderate consumption.

In modern society, many people enjoy a level of material abundance that would have been unimaginable throughout most of human history. It is widely assumed that material circumstances strongly affect human happiness. However, as the example of the "poor little rich girl" suggests, objective outcomes and happiness are not perfectly correlated.

Consider moving from an apartment with a view of a car park to one with a view of the ocean shoreline. Instead of waking up to engine noise you can watch the sunrise every morning.

Though pleasure conferred by the beachside view diminishes over time until gazing upon waves crashing into the shoreline brings no more pleasure than formerly derived from gazing upon cars parked on asphalt.

During the late 1990s, Michael Eysenck, a British psychologist, wrote of a "hedonic treadmill theory". The theory compares the pursuit of happiness to a person on a treadmill. Put another way, human happiness remains stationary, despite efforts or interventions to advance it.

Efforts to increase consumer happiness through consumption might be wasted, or worse, lead to lower consumer satisfaction.

Candy Crush Saga

At one point attracting 93 million users, Candy Crush Saga has proved one of the most popular games on Facebook, Android, and iOS. In the game, players complete levels by swapping coloured pieces of candy on a game board to make a match of three or more of the same colour, eliminating those candies from the board and replacing them with new ones.

Key to the game's success, each board has various goals that must be completed within a fixed number of moves or within a limited amount of time, such as a certain score or collecting a specific number of a type of candy.

This feature takes advantage of a phenomenon called "hedonic adaptation"; the fact that we get used to nice things over time until they no longer anywhere near as pleasurable. It's the reason why your new car is a lot less exciting after 6 months of ownership, why a new song gets old, and why the fourth piece of pizza isn't nearly as appealing as the first.

Candy Crush Saga counter-intuitively limits how much you can play the game in one day. While traditional video games give players the option of gorging on a game until they burn out on it and move on, Candy Crush Saga cleverly forces us to avoid that behaviour.

If you are forced to take frequent breaks, you will get more enjoyment out of the game when you do get to play. Thus, you will develop a Candy Crush Saga habit spread over a longer period of time, which gives the developer, King, more chances convert you on in-app

purchases or convince you to send game invites to your friends.

Television Commercials (part 1)

In the UK publicly funded television channels, namely the BBC, show no commercial advertisements between programmes. Viewers will often cite that they would prefer to watch television programs without commercials. Nevertheless, commercially funded channels still enjoy high ratings in the UK.

A group of researchers proposed that commercial interruptions can actually improve the television-viewing experience (Nelson & Meyvis, 2009). In the first of a number of experiments they carried out, participants were asked to watch an episode of a television programme, Taxi.

The programme was shown to half of the participants exactly as it was aired in 2005, including the commercial advertisements. The commercials were local advertisements (Jewelry Factory Store, the Law Office of Michael Brownstein) as well as network promotions for television shows. The remaining half of participants watched the same episode, however this time with the commercials removed. Both groups were told the scenarios in advance.

Before watching the show, all participants were asked to estimate whether they thought they would prefer watching this episode over a similar program, Happy Days, using an 11-point relative preference scale from -5 (definitely prefer Happy Days) to +5 (definitely prefer Taxi).

After watching the episode, participants were again asked to compare the episode to Happy Days using an identical 11-point scale.

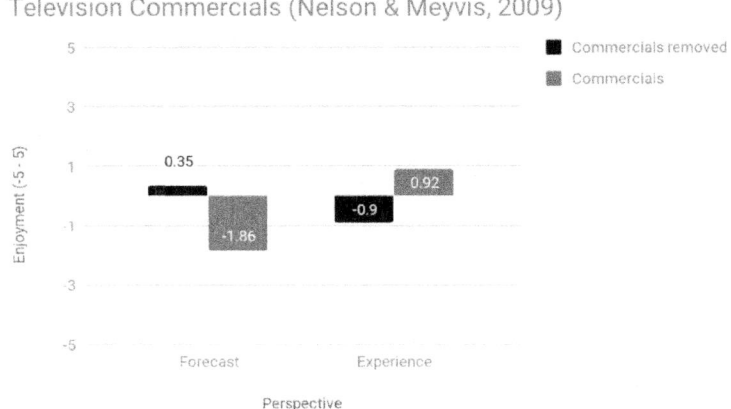

Television Commercials (Nelson & Meyvis, 2009)

As predicted, those who knew they would be watching the programme with the advertisements removed forecasted greater enjoyment afterwards (M = 0.35) than those who know it would be interrupted by adverts (M = -1.86).

However, after watching the show, the scores completely reversed. Those who had watched the show in one sitting reported lower enjoyment (M = -0.90) than those who interrupted whilst watching by adverts (M = 0.92) who now reported more enjoyment from this show than Happy Days. The forecasters did not predict the effect of adaptation, nor did they
predict the moderating role of the disruption.

Interrupting the Taxi episode made the program more enjoyable. The commercials disrupted the participant's adaptation to "normal", thus helping to maintain an overall high level of enjoyment.

Over time we get familiar with something; a TV show, the food we're eating, our jobs. By introducing interruptions to remove adaptation can significantly boost ongoing satisfaction, even if we don't think it will.

Television Commercials (part 2)

It is widely accepted that we, as humans, tend to dwell on negative events more than we do positive equivalents (see: negativity bias). When a significant negative life interruption occurs, for example losing a job, some might think; "I'll never be able to find another job as good again".

Clearly, in some situations, this sentiment might be correct, though oftentimes life will return to normality within time. The concept of the "hedonistic treadmill" argues just this; that following an interruption, positive or negative, we'll move back towards normal over time. The same group of researchers considered this theory and added a measure of time to their experiment (Nelson & Meyvis, 2009).

Participants in this experiment first watched two 3-minute nature documentaries (one about bison and one about deserts). Half of the participants watched the two documentaries in succession (continuous condition), while the other half watched the first half of each documentary, followed by the second half of each documentary (disrupted condition).

After watching both documentaries, participants reported their enjoyment of the documentaries on a 9-point scale from 1 (did not enjoy) to 9 (really enjoyed).

Television Commercials (part 2) (Nelson & Meyvis, 2009)

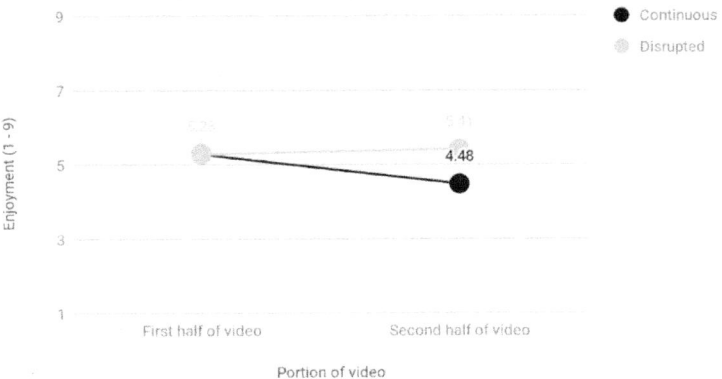

Those who watched the videos continuously enjoyed the second half marginally less than the first (M = 5.28 vs M = 4.48) whereas people who watched the disrupted videos enjoyed the second half slightly more than the first half (M = 5.28 vs M = 5.41).

As before, participants experienced adaptation when television programs were shown continuously but not when the programs had been disrupted.

Additional research has shown that adaptation effects happen both in the short-term, including commercial breaks, and long-term, during major life events for example (Tella, 2007). In both cases people adapt relatively quickly to experiences, thus reducing their enjoyment from it.

Interruptions to positive events can cause an immediate (or expected) drop in reported enjoyment, but after the interruption has ended and we return to the experience, we quickly return to a baseline of normal. In many cases, our enjoyment is actually heightened after the interruption as it diminishes the

effects of adaptation. For those who struggle with routines due to hedonic adaptation, it can often be advantageous to break them up with interruptions.

Noise Pollution

The first two experiments considered positive experiences. Though researchers pondered if we adapted to negative events in the same way, and if breaking them up had the opposite effect to before, that is making them worse (Nelson & Meyvis, 2008).

In an experiment, participants were seated at a computer workstation, asked to put on headphones, and told that they would be listening to a brief sound clip of a vacuum cleaner. The participants were split into 3 groups:

1. the first group listened to only 5 seconds of the vacuum cleaner;
2. the second group listened to 40 seconds;
3. and the final group listened to 40 seconds, followed by a 5-second break, and then another 5 seconds of the vacuum cleaner.

All participants were then to compare the last 5-seconds of the vacuum cleaner clip to another irritating noise, a 5-second sample of a drilling sound that was played to them immediately after the first clip. They reported their preference between the two sounds on a 201-point scale from −100 (definitely prefer the vacuum) to +100 (definitely prefer the drill).

Noise Pollution (Nelson & Meyvis, 2008)

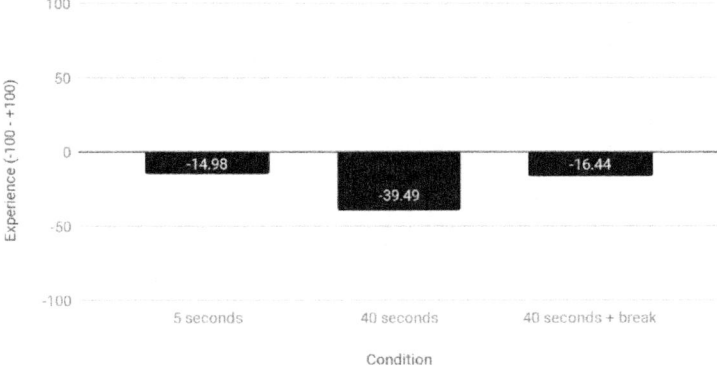

The researchers expected that people would adapt to the noise and therefore find it less aversive after 40 seconds than after only 5 seconds. They were correct. Participants experiencing the noise continuously for 40 seconds judged the last 5 seconds to be less aversive (M = −39.49) than people experiencing just the first 5 seconds (M = −14.98) or people experiencing the 5 seconds after a break (M = −16.44).

These results indicate that though people often want to break up negative experiences, this is not always a wise decision. Whereas listening to the noise for an extended period made the noise less aversive due to hedonic adaptation, inserting a break made the noise just as aversive as it had been initially -- the break disrupted the adaptation process.

We adapt to both positive and negative experiences. However, unlike interruptions to positive experiences that can result in them being enhanced, negative experiences are actually made worse by interruptions because we cannot adapt to them.

Musical break

Interruptions can take a number of forms. Students are often advised to take regular study breaks to retain focus. Such breaks often take the form of an activity that is enjoyed by the student. Though life is not always of simplistic. Occasionally we are disrupted by unexpected, sometimes negative events.

The following experiment investigated possible contrast effects by inserting pleasant and aversive breaks (Nelson & Meyvis, 2008). Researchers split participants into four groups;

1. In the continuous condition, participants listened to 20 seconds of silence, followed by 180 seconds of vacuum noise.
2. In the positive condition, participants listened to 180 seconds of vacuum noise but were interrupted after 160 seconds by 20 seconds of classical piano music (Glenn Gould performing Bach's Goldberg Variations).
3. In the neutral condition, participants listened to 180 seconds of vacuum noise but were interrupted after 160 seconds by 20 seconds of silence.
4. In the negative condition, participants listened to 180 seconds of vacuum noise but were interrupted after 160 seconds by a 20-second recording of a child practising scales on a violin.

After the experience, participants evaluated it on a nine-point scale anchored by 1 (not unpleasant) to 9 (extremely unpleasant) and stated their relative preference between listening to the vacuum cleaner noise and listening to a drilling noise on a 201-point scale from -100 (prefer vacuum cleaner) to 100 (prefer drill). The two measures were standardised and combined them into a single irritation measure between -1 (no irritation) and 1 (maximum irritation).

Musical Break (Nelson & Meyvis, 2008)

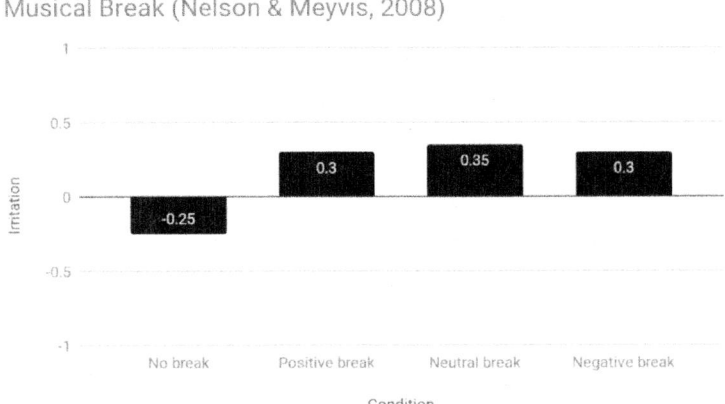

All three breaks (silence, piano music, and violin practice) disrupted adaptation to the vacuum noise and the participants reported an increased intensity of the irritation (M = 0.35, M = 0.3 and M = 0.3 respectively) preferring the drilling sound. Where adaptation to the vacuum was allowed to continue the participants reported much lower levels of irritation (M = -0.25) signalling a preference for the vacuum of the drill.

The experiment was reversed using positive stimuli, as opposed to a negative vacuum sound, in which similar findings resulted.

Both experiments showed breaks regardless of their valence, limit the effects of adaptation, improving enjoyment for positive events but having the opposite effect for negative events, increasing their intensity.

Chocolate Bars

In the western world, food is plentiful. Though the results suggest that the fifth slice of pizza, or in the experiment below, the piece of chocolate, does not always taste as good as the first.

In a two-week experiment, researchers looked at the effects of limiting chocolate consumption on a group of participants (Quoidbach & Dunn, 2013). The group of participants were split into three groups:

1. In the restricted access condition, participants were instructed not to eat any chocolate for a week, until they returned to the lab.
2. In the abundant access condition, the experimenter gave participants approximately 2 pounds (900 grams) of chocolate (one large bar per day) with the instruction to eat as much as they comfortably could over the course of the week.
3. In the control condition, participants did not receive any specific instructions related to their chocolate consumption.

When they returned to the lab, all participants were then asked to taste a piece of chocolate before rating how much they savoured it on a scale from 1 (not at all) to 7 (a great deal).

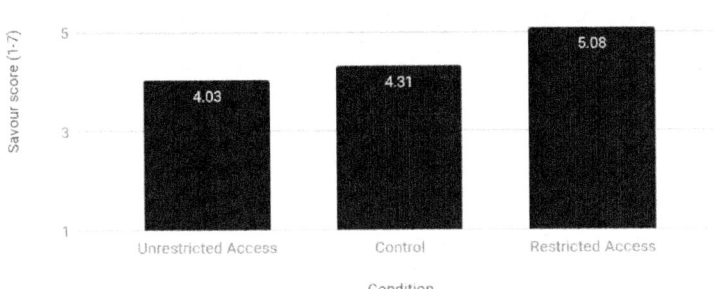

Chocolate Bars (Quoidbach & Dunn, 2013)

Participants in the restricted access condition savoured the chocolate more (M = 5.08) than those in the abundant access condition (M = 4.31) or control condition (M = 4.31). The participants in the latter two groups did not differ from each other, suggesting that when restrictions are in place the anticipation of the next opportunity to enjoy the experience will be heightened.

What we want isn't always what makes us happiest, especially in situations where consumption can be hard to moderate.

Product Gems

1. **Consider service interruptions for more pleasant experiences...**
   If you're trying to maximize consumer enjoyment, it would be sensible to insert short breaks (e.g., insert several pauses when serving the chef's tasting menu).

2. **... but not for unpleasant ones**
   Similar reasoning can be applied to unpleasant experiences. Many service experiences either are mostly unpleasant (e.g., medical procedures) or have a nontrivial unpleasant component (e.g., waiting on the tarmac for a flight to take off). Indeed, despite our preferences, it may be ill-advised to offer patients the opportunity to take a break in a moderately unpleasant medical procedure.

3. **Provide multiple experiences**
   Consider a salesperson providing a demonstration of a pleasant product or service experience. Rather than providing consumers with one extended test drive, it may be more effective to provide customers with a sequence of interrupted product experiences. Each interruption disrupts the adaptation process and enables consumers to experience again the thrill of the initial experience.

4. **Find ways to keep customers in a state of slight but permanent hunger**
   Getting the right balance through the limiting of access is a challenge, especially when people are asked for their opinion. Consider maintaining a steady cadence of new releases so your consumers are always ready to consume more. Do

you enjoy a television series more when it's released weekly or in one go?

5. **What people think they want isn't always what will make them happiest**

   Striking the right balance can be a challenge when imposing limitations. Do it thoughtfully and carefully to build the appetite for a product. For example, the slow, strategic release of a piece of media or chapters of digital content can help build anticipation and a positive frenzy.

6. **Consider inbuilt consumer-imposed restrictions**

   While customers will often want too much of a good thing, they are often receptive to recommendations about what's best for them. For example, Microsoft allows parents (or players) to impose screen time limits on their Xbox One console.

7. **Don't overcompensate for negative interruptions**

   Over time our feelings return to a baseline normal level as the effects of the negative (or positive) event weaken. Negative events might actually increase overall satisfaction. Carefully understand the cost a negative experience has on a customer, how long it will take to return to normal and the benefit of investing in an immediate resolution.

14. Negativity Bias

We have a greater recall of unpleasant experiences than positive ones

We pay more attention or give more weight to negative experiences over neutral or positive experiences. Consumers react by buying less on bad news, but sadly don't buy more when hearing good, so be mindful of current sentiment!

Growing up I could not really fault my parents. They would, frustratingly as a teenager, insist on being early for events. Clocks would be set with military precision, routes to locations researched days in advance and any required preparation done the night before, at the latest.

Except for one school trip. It started with some misplaced car keys, followed by a wrong turn, a traffic jam, and ultimately arriving at school to see the coach pulling out of the school car park. Other schools might have phoned the coach driver to turn around. My no-nonsense headmaster did not run one of those other schools. Lateness was punishable with a day in the classroom, instead of a prized geography trip to the beach.

Every holiday provides me with a prime opportunity to remind them, and others, about their tardiness on this occasion. Admittedly there was little they could do, fifteen years ago. When I bring it up, they quickly question me about all the times they weren't late. I can't remember any specifics -- a prime example of my negativity bias.

Our brains are wired to dwell on the time's life has not gone to plan, not on the countless times it did. We have a tendency to focus more on the negatives than the positives - in ourselves, in others (particularly our parents!), in our circumstances; in the past, in the present and when forecasting the future.

As a result, negative information prompts us to take action much more swiftly than similar positive information would.

Online Reviews

In the age of the internet, reputations are almost never a blank slate. Consumers are surrounded by online reviews thanks to other consumers who've gone to the trouble of posting opinions about products and services online.

Though there is a systematic problem with many online reviews — they tend to over-represent the most extreme negative views.

Typically, if a consumer absolutely hates a product, they are more likely to share their experience with others including, ever more increasingly, via online reviews. Whereas those that have positive or indifferent views of products often find sharing a review not worth the time or effort.

Polarisation of product reviews can be a real challenge for any retailer. Reviews have a large sway on a customer's decision to purchase. Not only do we look to see what others have purchased (see: social default bias), we are also looking to their experiences when making deciding on what to buy.

When we stumble upon a negative evaluation, it tends to stick out. One negative review could easily dissuade a potential customer from a purchase, even if the negative review holds little credibility and is countered by many contradicting positive reviews, as is often the case.

Not only are consumers more likely to report negative experiences, but bad feedback also has more impact on other customers than equally positive feedback does.

Psychology Research

Psychologists, too, suffer from a negativity bias. Researchers analysed 17,000 Polish publications on psychology and coded them as positive or negative (Czapinski, 1985).

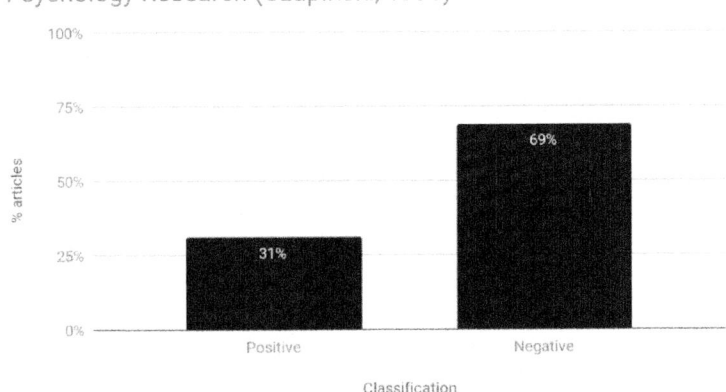

Psychology Research (Czapinski, 1985)

69% of the articles were focused on negative issues, whereas only 31% were focused on positive issues.

The researchers proposed that psychologists focused too much on understanding the bad rather than the good. A recent review paper by Baumeister and colleagues has highlighted the many research areas in which this "bad over good" bias is evident (Baumeister et al., 2001).

We have a natural tendency to focus on negative experiences over positive experiences.

Life Changes

As demonstrated we have more of a focus on negativity, though perhaps most detrimental to our wellbeing, it is often the case that we spend most time dwelling retrospectively on negative events.

In an experiment testing this phenomenon, researchers interviewed three groups of people (Brickman et al., 1978); people who had won a lottery, people who had been paralyzed in an accident, and people who had not recently experienced any such major life event.

For a measure of general happiness, respondents were asked to rate how happy they were now (not at this moment, but at this stage of their life). They were also asked to rate how happy they were before winning (for the lottery group); before the accident (for the victim group); or 6 months ago (for the control group). Finally, each group was asked to rate how happy they expected to be in a couple of years.

All ratings were made on 6-point scales ranging from 0 for "not at all" to 5 for "very much."

Life Changes (Brickman et al., 1978)

Lottery winners and those who had experienced no significant life changes over the period saw happiness level increase steadily over time (M = 3.77, M = 4.00, M = 4.20 and M = 3.32, M = 3.82, M = 4.14). In both cases, expected future happiness was higher than their reported happiness at the time (see: optimism bias).

The victims continued to compare their current situation with how their lives had been before the accident (M = 2.96 vs M = 4.41) (unlike lottery winners, who did not seem to spend much time thinking how their lives had improved from the bygone days of relative poverty).

Importantly though the decrease in happiness from before the event to the present in the victim condition was significantly greater (M = -1.45) than the increase seen for the lottery winners condition (M = 0.2).

We place significantly more weight on negative information than we do for equally positive information.

Product Evaluations (part 1)

Another experiment, this time examining the effects of sentiment on product evaluation, tested the extent that positive and negative information can have on consumers (Lalwani, 2006).

Participants were told they would be shown a number of products and services (airline tickets, apartments, cars, shampoos, hotels) alongside reviews provided by a well known company, Consumer Reports, who curate real consumer reviews.

Depending on the condition they were in, participants were shown positive, negative, or neutral reviews alongside the products.

After reading the information and reviews for each product, they were then asked to evaluate it on a 0 to 10 scale anchored by "very bad" to "very good."

Product Evaluations (part 1) (Lalwani, 2006)

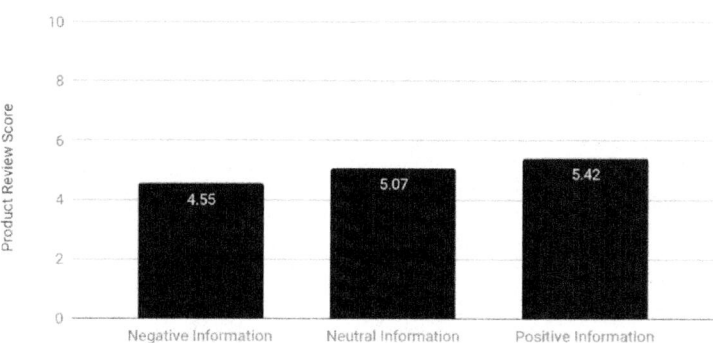

Unsurprisingly, participants in the positive goal condition evaluated the products more favourably (M = 5.60) than those in the negative goal condition (M = 4.86) and those in the neutral condition (M = 5.07).

The evaluations in the neutral and positive conditions were not significantly different when compared to the negative condition, again suggesting greater salience of negative information.

We place greater emphasis on negative information in evaluating products. Bad reviews or a poor pre-sales experience can instantly result in a lost sale, however positive information, sadly, does not have the opposite effect.

Product Evaluations (part 2)

With a proliferation of skewed reviews and ever more increasingly, paid product reviews, many consumers have become sceptical as to their credibility. As such, researchers wanted to test if factual, diagnostic information about products had the same effect on consumers compared to instances where evaluations could be deemed as subjective (Lalwani, 2006).

Again, participants were shown a range of products alongside evaluations from the company, Consumer Reports. This time the participants were split into two groups with half shown positive evaluations, and the other half shown negative product evaluations.

In this experiment, the evaluations shown to participants were clearly objective containing only diagnostic and factual information. For example, the hotel evaluation listed attributes including; "had 24 hours on-site security", "had 24 hours surveillance cameras above all doors", and "was not close to public transportation".

After reading the information and reviews for each product, they were then asked to evaluate it on a 0 to 10 scale anchored by "very bad" to "very good."

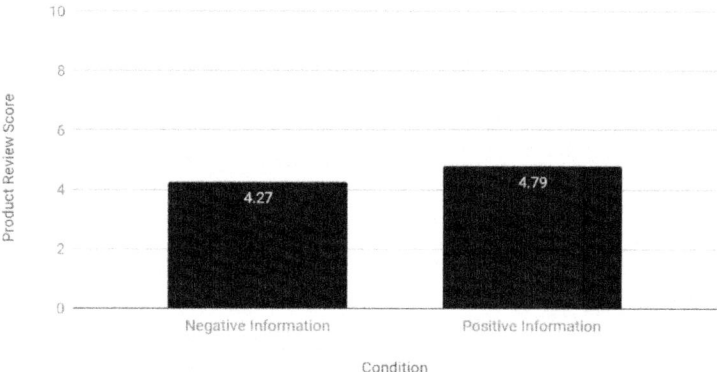

Product Evaluations (part 2) (Lalwani, 2006)

In lieu of a neutral condition, researchers expected the neutral level to sit below the middle possible evaluation score of 5 (between 0 - 10). Put another way, it was expected that the positive reviews would not be as stimulating to participants as the negative reviews.

Indeed, the positive evaluation condition led to scores slightly lower than 5 (M = 4.79), whilst the negative reviews significantly influenced the participant's evaluations of the products downwards (M = 4.27).

Even factual, positive information does little to convince us. Conversely, we are significantly influenced by factual negative information.

Good News, Bad News

In a real-world scenario, researchers examined popular economic and financial news covering the Australian labour market, monetary policy, and financial markets (Nguyen & Claus, 2013).

To test consumer reaction to good and bad news periods, the researchers reviewed the daily rise and fall of the Standard & Poor's 500, often abbreviated as the S&P 500, an American stock market index based on the market capitalizations of 500 large companies between January 1996 and December 2011.

They then correlated the performance of the index against a Consumer Sentiment Index (CSI) constructed from a monthly survey of Australian households consisting of questions on the economy, household financial conditions and whether it is a good time to buy major household items.

The study split the respondents based on incomes; low-income households and high-income households.

Good News, Bad News (Nguyen & Claus, 2013)

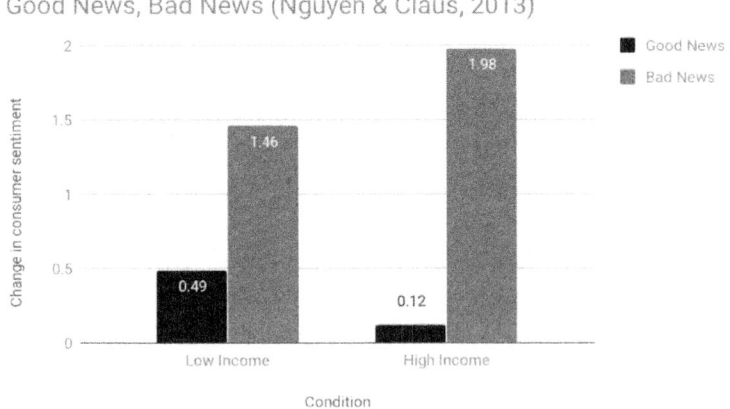

As expected, high-income households reacted stronger to bad market news than those on lower incomes (M = 1.98 and M = 1.46, respectively). It is interesting to note that lower income households acted on good news about the market more strongly (M = 0.49 and M = 0.12, respectively). Perhaps suggesting a stronger interest from lower-income households to consider financial investments when times are good.

Clearly when we have a vested interest in something we are more likely to take action, especially financial based investments. However, it is when we are presented with negative information, like poor financial performance, that we are most likely to take action. If the news is good, we're more likely to continue to follow the status quo (see: status quo bias). This attitude is summed up by the adage; don't fix it if it isn't broken.

We are more likely to take action when faced with negative information when we have a vested interest in the outcome.

Product Gems

1. **Monitor consumer experience**
   Make sure you're fully aware of the overall sentiment of consumers. If there are areas of your product or service that receive consistently negative feedback, be proactive and focus on making improvements.

2. **Emphasise positive events**
   When consumers are faced with a decision, it is important to counteract the negativity bias by placing a significant amount of emphasis on the positive benefits of a choice. We take more convincing than we think.

3. **Objective information is not (always) the solution**
   Positive, objective evaluations of products are indeed helpful, perhaps from an independent researcher, but as shown, their effect on consumers is not always as powerful as you might believe. Beware of marketing spend on this type of activity.

4. **Watch out for negative events**
   Just one damaging story about your brand or a negative product review has the power to destroy an otherwise perfect reputation. Make sure you handle negative events with humility and in a timely fashion.

5. **Use negative events to your advantage**
   If your competitor has suffered from some bad news stories recently consider taking advantage of it. Perhaps you could highlight some of the reasons why you have a superior offering relevant to the news stories. Though be careful, wallowing in

someone else misfortune can have the opposite effect on consumers.

6. **Motivate consumers with negativity**
   When consumers have a vested interest in something, they are more likely to take action, especially when negative information is presented. Consider warning users of the negative outcomes that might result should they fail to take action (see: status quo bias).

(If you did or *did not* enjoy this chapter, feel free to leave a review on Amazon.)

15. Bottom Dollar Effect

We rate products negatively when they exhaust our budgets

When we buy a product that exhausts our remaining budget, the negative emotions associated with parting with money are transferred onto the product, thereby influencing its ratings.

Ask a group students about finances and it's likely they'll break into a sweat. I speak from experience. As a student, money was tight. My bank balance rarely stretched further than a diet of Ramen noodles for dinner each evening.

A part-time job offered some relief, if only temporarily. The money I'd earn regularly funded nights out where I would drink my wages twice as fast as it took me to earn them (see: present bias). To my parent's relief, I'd always leave some money aside for some more sensible treats.

One such treat involved a night out to the cinema to watch The Dark Knight, a film that, at the time of writing scores an impressive 9/10 on IMDb. Not wanting to spoil the plot, the late Heath Ledger's iconic portrayal of the Joker in the film earned critical acclaim. Controversially, I'm not sure I'd rate it quite as highly.

Jumping back in time, the trip to the cinema was three days before I was due to be paid. The ticket cost me everything left in my account, a mere £10, a sum made even more expensive when you consider the ticket cost included a generous student discount.

As the movie started, an iconic bank robbery scene, I started to mentally run through what I should have spent the money on. Namely, dinner; more Ramen noodles. As I continued to stew on my decision, the end credits started rolling. The films two-and-a-half-hour run-time, costing me roughly £4 per hour, saw me distracted for the duration, ultimately dissatisfied with the film.

The bottom dollar effect refers to the tendency of consumers facing financial hardship to transfer negative emotions associated with their hardship onto the last few products or services that, at the margin, they perceive as straining their budget.

The unfortunate consequence of this effect is that consumers may become dissatisfied with a purchase based not on their actual satisfaction with the goods or services purchased, but instead, on the timing of that purchase and the resources they happened to have available at that time.

Spotify

My teenage years saw the transition from physical music formats dominating the market with digital music products replacing them, including the birth of the iconic Apple iPod. I now look back on CD's somewhat nostalgically (see: nostalgia effect) but can't imagine going back to a world where I'm unable to stream millions of songs on-demand.

Part of the nostalgia for CD's was the buying experience. My parents, who grew up on vinyl describe this experience with even more vividness; the smells of the freshly pressed disc, the artwork printed on the sleeve, and the soft crackling as the record spun for the first time. Though these nostalgic experiences were comparatively more expensive. Spending £10 on an album quickly added up. Friends who are real music lovers recall spending hundreds each month on music.

For me, buying an album containing many songs I didn't even like left me questioning my purchase afterwards. When I was saving for something larger, the feeling of regret loomed even larger. Subscription-based products, including Spotify, have reduced these feeling almost entirely.

Charging a comparatively low monthly fee, costing slightly more than a CD, makes the recurring purchase each month seem negligible and is much less likely to exhaust or constrain ones' budget.

Negative emotions associated with hardship are transferred onto the products or services we perceive are straining our budgets.

Weekly Budgets

Previous research has found we have a greater aversion to spending when the costs incurred exhaust our budgetary resources. However, some purchases just can't be avoided, or we lack the self-control for restraint (see: present bias).

Early research of the bottom dollar effect explored what effect constrained budgets had on our aversion to spending (Soster et al., 2014). In one such experiment, participants were split into two groups;

1. Budget absent condition: Participants were given no information about what their imaginary weekly budget had been spent on. Half of the group were simply told to imagine they had $10 left to spend, with the other half being told $88 remained in their budget.
2. Budget present condition: Participants were given a detailed imaginary budget showing each expense listed, how much was spent, and how much remained in the budget. Similarly to the budget absent group, the remaining balances for the participants were shown as either $10 or $88.

All participants then reported how they would feel about purchasing a $10 movie ticket. That is, those in the spending to zero condition considered a purchase that would reduce a $10 balance to $0, while participants who were not spending to zero evaluated a purchase that reduced an $88 balance to $78.

Each participant then their aversion to spending rating their agreement with the statement: "I ought to save this $10.00

and not spend it," on a 5-point Likert scale from 1 (disagree) to 5 (agree).

Weekly Budgets (Soster et al., 2014)

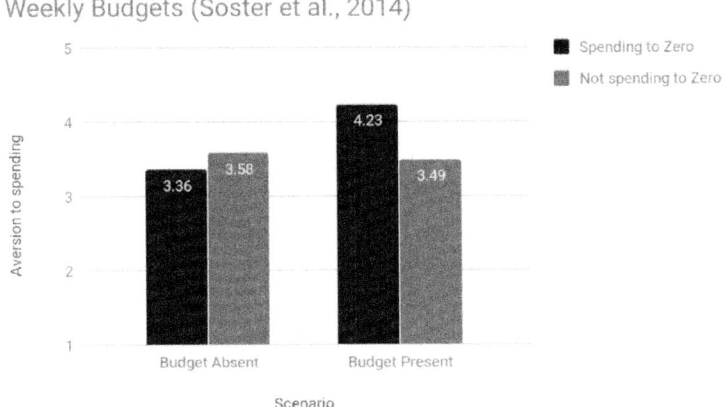

When an explicit budget was diminished, spending aversion was higher for those spending to zero (M = 4.23) than for those with money remaining after the purchase (M = 3.49). However, when no explicit budget was diminished, the effect attenuated. That is, no differences in aversion arose whether the $10 cost exhausted resources (M = 3.36) or not (M = 3.58).

Consumers' aversion to spending resources is greater for costs that exhaust budgetary resources. The effect diminishes if no explicit budget is present. This supports the notion that budget balances, or mental accounts, are used as reference points when considering expenditures, in turn influencing the psychological burden of paying (Kahneman and Tversky, 1979; Thaler, 1980).

Film Credits (part 1)

The first study suggests that aversion to spending is greater when the costs incurred exhaust budgetary resources. Researchers argued that this aversion influences the satisfaction of our decisions (Soster et al., 2014).

To test this theory, participants in an experiment were told to imagine they had purchased credits (described as being worth $0.30 each) to spend on films that cost 10 credits ($3.00) each. The researchers split the participants into two groups:

1. Bottom dollar spending condition: participants' budgets were initially funded with 30 credits ($9) so that the purchase of a third film resulted in exhausted budgets.
2. Non–bottom dollar condition: participants' budgets were funded with 50 credits ($15) so that purchasing the third film did not exhaust budgets.

Each participant was then instructed to purchase and watch three films. Before participants purchased each film, they were reminded of their current budget balance, the cost to purchase the film, and the balance that would remain after their purchase.

Participants then evaluated each film they had watched, responding to the following statement: "Please rate your feelings about the film you just watched," assessed on a 9-point scale from 1 (extremely dissatisfied) to 9 (extremely satisfied).

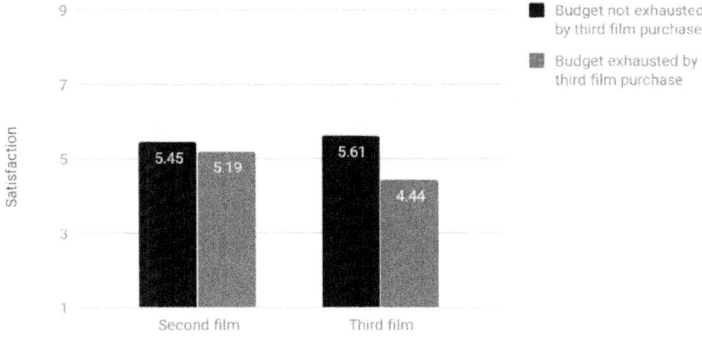

Film Credits (part 1) (Soster et al., 2014)

After watching the second film participants in both the exhausted and non-exhausted budget conditions gave similar satisfaction ratings for the films (M = 5.45 and M = 5.19, respectively).

Fascinatingly, it was found that the people who'd exhausted their budget by the third film were less satisfied with it (M = 4.44), compared to those whose budget hadn't run out (M = 5.61) whose ratings were fairly similar to those given to the second film.

Buying something when our budget balance is relatively low is likely to be more painful than when our remaining budget is high.

Film Credits (part 2)

Prior research suggests that the difficulty ascribed to earning resources can influence the pain of spending (Bagchi & Block, 2011). If, as hypothesised, the pain of paying is associated with the bottom dollar effect, when a consumer finds it difficult to earn resources, the bottom dollar effect should be more pronounced than for those who perceive earning as easy.

Researchers conducted an experiment where participants earned credits that they used to purchase short films (Soster et al., 2014). To earn the credits, participants were required to perform a series of tasks that required sorting lists of items into four categories (e.g., animals, Simpsons episodes, cities, or diseases).

The participants were split into two groups;

1. Easy task condition: Participants sorted only four items into the categories
2. Hard tasks condition: Participants were required to sort 28 items into the categories

For each task completed, participants were given 10 credits.

Each short film cost 10 credits to purchase. Participants in the exhausting budget condition completed three tasks so that purchasing the third film would exhaust their budget. Those in the not exhausting condition completed four tasks so that the purchase of the third film would not fully deplete their budgets.

Across conditions, participants saw the same three films, in the same order, responding to a direct measure of satisfaction using a 9-point bipolar scale from 1 (extremely dissatisfied) to 9 (extremely satisfied).

Film Credits (part 2) (Soster et al., 2014)

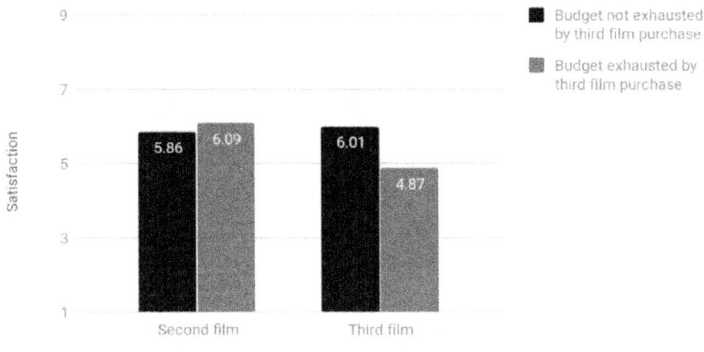

In support of their hypotheses, the results revealed that, when earning was difficult, those who had exhausted their budgets were less satisfied (M = 4.87) than those who had not (M = 6.01). However, when earning was easy, no differences in satisfaction emerged on the basis of budget status.

In addition, when budgets were exhausted, those in the difficult earning condition were less satisfied (M = 4.87) than those in the easy condition (M = 6.09). When budgets were not exhausted, there was no difference in satisfaction based on earning in the hard and easy conditions (M = 6.01 and M = 5.86, respectively).

The pain of payment increases the harder it is to replenish our budgets. Consumers who find it hard to replenish their budgets suffer heightened bottom dollar effects when a product exhausts their existing budget.

Film Credits (part 3)

People typically get paid once a month or once every two weeks. As a result, the closer we are to exhausting our budget over income periods, it is logical to think we will wait until our next paycheck instead of exhausting our budget in the interim (see: fresh start effect). Though as irrational creatures we're far from logical when it comes to time (see: present bias).

In a follow-up experiment in the series, the researchers used a similar scenario (Soster et al., 2014). In this experiment, budgets were not filled with credits, but dollars. All participants were told that they had started the week with an entertainment budget of $60 and then considered a series of purchases, one by one, that required them to calculate each decline.

For example, they were asked:

> *"If you spend $4 on music downloads, how much remains in your budget?"*

This purchasing simulation was repeated for multiple purchases until those in the exhausting budget condition had $2 left, and those in the non-exhausting condition had $13.

Next, a replenishment timing manipulation was introduced. Participants were split into three groups:

1. Unknown condition: participants were given no information about replenishment
2. Near-future condition: participants were told they would receive $60 "tomorrow morning,"

3. Far-future condition: participants were told they would receive $60 "in 6 more days."

Participants then considered the target purchase, a $2 online film. The purchase would leave those in the exhausted budget condition with a remaining balance of $0.

After making the $2 purchase, all participants were then asked to indicate their satisfaction with the film using a 7-point scale from 1 (extremely dissatisfied) to 7 (extremely satisfied).

Film Credits (part 3) (Soster et al., 2014)

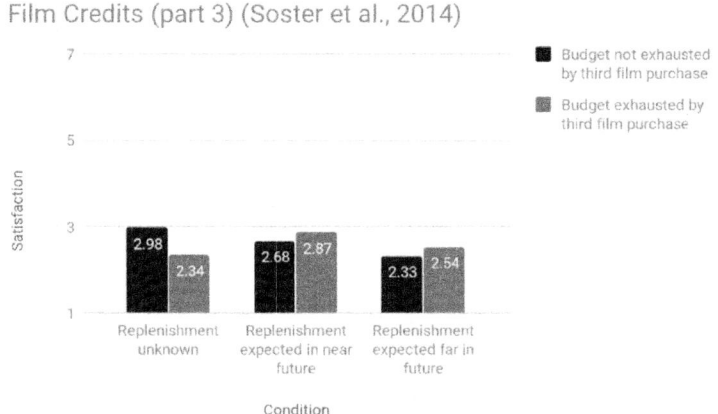

For participants given no replenishment information, the bottom dollar effect arose, as it did in the first two experiments. Participants with exhausting budgets were less satisfied (M = 2.34) than those with non-exhausting budgets (M = 2.98).

For those with exhausting budgets, no differences in satisfaction arose whether replenishment timing was unknown (M = 2.34) or 6 days away (M = 2.54). However, satisfaction was higher for those with exhausting budgets when they were told they would receive replenishment the next day (M = 2.87). **In situations where budgets are exhausting, perceptions of expedited replenishment will reduce the pain associated with spending one's bottom dollar and increase satisfaction with the purchase.**

Additional contrasts revealed the opposite pattern for participants with non-exhausting budgets. Satisfaction was the same whether replenishment timing was unknown (M = 2.98) or expected in the near future (M = 2.68). However, satisfaction was significantly lower for participants told that replenishment was far (M = 2.33) than for those given no replenishment information. **Satisfaction may be lower for individuals with non-exhausted budgets if they perceive that budget replenishment will not occur until the distant future.**

Decreased satisfaction may also arise prior to bottom dollar spending when other factors increase payment pain, including lack of immediate fund replenishment.

Product Gems

1. **Timing is key**
   Marketing a product may be more effective if timed at a period when consumer budgets are less likely to be exhausted, such as at the start of a month (see: Fresh Start Effect), rather than the end. We humans also find parting with money to be psychologically-painful (e.g. Prelec & Loewenstein, 1998), and this is said to be affected by changes in our remaining budget.

2. **Payday matters**
   Marketing promotional offers and discounts may be more effective when budgets are likely to be exhausted, such as towards the end of the month. If possible, try and understand when your users are paid, a date that typically falls on standardised dates within a country, and adjust marketing spend around these periods. Similarly, if you offer a subscription-based product, consider allowing the consumer to adjust their billing dates around these dates.

3. **Understand segment behaviours**
   However, that the effect is reduced when budgets are said to be replenished immediately suggests that marketing just before this time can still increase sales. The key here is to identify your target audience and make an estimate of when their budgets are likely to be exhausted and replenished.

4. **Consider pricing promotions when budgets are exhausted**
   The end of the month — when more consumers are likely to be spending their bottom dollars — may be the time to use special pricing incentives — like

surprise coupons — to reduce the pain of paying, not only to make the sale, but also to increase satisfaction.

5. **Know the mental account**

   This research is based on earlier findings that we essentially chunk our money into mental accounts (e.g. Thaler, 1985). For example, we may treat our salary as being different from a monthly bonus. Knowing that people actually categorise their spending behaviour, you should understand what mental account your product is likely to draw from. While a consumer's overall budget might be high, their remaining balance in individual categories might be on their bottom dollars.

6. **Be considerate with feedback requests**

   There may also be an opportunity to delay any explicit request for a product review until after consumer budgets are likely to have been replenished.

7. **As consumers, we can help ourselves**

   Finally, the insight has strong implications for consumers themselves. Allowing the pain of parting with money to influence our product ratings can make us less satisfied with our purchase.

   Therefore, making more purchases when budgets are replenished can help us avoid such emotions and increase overall satisfaction with the products we buy.

16. Conclusion

In the same way that diamonds are abundant on earth, so too are the number of biases we as humans fall victim to. Wikipedia lists over one hundred cognitive biases from the ambiguity effect, our tendency to avoid options for which missing information makes the probability seem "unknown", to the zero-sum bias, a bias whereby a situation is incorrectly perceived to be like a zero-sum game (i.e., one-person gains at the expense of another).

Having spent many hours reading academic literature and exploring the way we make decisions, my irrational brain still keeps me from getting it right much of the time. Our inherent biases will always affect our decisions, behaviours, and memories.

While you might put down this book thinking of ways to turn things into a science experiment, remember, it's a process. Implementing all the *gems* in this book won't, on its own, lead to the next Patagonia, Amazon, or Netflix. But it will help you take a step in the right direction to build products people love.

Acknowledgements

This book would not have been possible without the support of my parents, Christopher and Alison, who allowed me to use their quiet study, now writing room, for many long nights spent researching and writing. Thank you for allowing me as a child to stay blissfully unaware of the world of adults for as long as you did, and then telling me the truth about it when I finally asked. A special mention to my Dad who inspired many of the examples cited in this book. You're not really the most irrational person I know, *most of the time*.

References

1. Fresh Start Effect

Dai, Hengchen & Milkman, Katherine & Riis, Jason. (2014). The Fresh Start Effect: Temporal Landmarks Motivate Aspirational Behavior. Management Science. 60. 2563-2582. 10.1287/mnsc.2014.1901.

L Alter, Adam & Hershfield, Hal. (2014). People search for meaning when they approach a new decade in chronological age: Table 1.. Proceedings of the National Academy of Sciences of the United States of America. 111. 10.1073/pnas.1415086111.

Vistr (2015). The best day to invoice customers to get paid faster.

2. Goal-gradient Effect

Cryder, Cynthia & Loewenstein, George & Seltman, Howard. (2013). Goal-gradient in helping behavior. Journal of Experimental Social Psychology. 49. 1078-1083. 10.1016/j.jesp.2013.07.003.

Nunes, Joseph & Drèze, Xavier. (2006). Your loyalty program is betraying you. Harvard business review. 84. 124-31; 150.

Kivetz, Ran & Urminsky, Oleg & Zheng, Yuhuang. (2006). The Goal-Gradient Hypothesis Resurrected: Purchase Acceleration, Illusionary Goal Progress, and Customer Retention. Journal of Marketing Research - J MARKET RES-CHICAGO. 43. 39-58. 10.1509/jmkr.43.1.39.

3. Motivating Uncertainty

Stearns, Stephen. (2000). Daniel Bernoulli (1738): Evolution and economics under risk. Journal of biosciences. 25. 221-8. 10.1007/BF02703928.

von Neumann, John & Morgenstern, Oskar. (1944). Theory of Games and Economic Behavior.

A. Kahneman, Daniel & N. Tversky, Amos. (1979). Prospect Theory: An Analysis of Decision Under Risk. Econometrica. 47. 263-91. 10.2307/1914185.

Shen, Luxi & Fishbach, Ayelet & Hsee, Christopher. (2015). The Motivating-Uncertainty Effect: Uncertainty Increases Resource Investment in the Process of Reward Pursuit. Journal of Consumer Research. 41. 1301-1315. 10.1086/679418.

List, John & Gneezy, Uri. (2006). Putting Behavioral Economics to Work: Testing for Gift Exchange in Labor Markets Using Field Experiments. Econometrica. 74. 1365-1384. 10.1111/j.1468-0262.2006.00707.x.

Zuckerman, Marvin. (2007). Sensation Seeking And Risky Behavior.

4. Zeigarnik Effect

Zeigarnik, Bluma. (1938). On finished and unfinished tasks.

McKinney, F. (1935). Studies in the retention of interrupted learning activities.. Journal of Comparative Psychology. 19. 265-296. 10.1037/h0056005.

ROSENZWEIG, SAUL & MASON, GWENDOLYN. (2011). An experimental study of memory in relation to the theory of repression. British Journal of Psychology. General Section. 24. 247 - 265. 10.1111/j.2044-8295.1934.tb00701.x.

5. Nostalgia Effect

Hepper, Erica & Ritchie, Timothy & Sedikides, Constantine & Wildschut, Tim. (2011). Odyssey's End: Lay Conceptions of Nostalgia Reflect Its Original Homeric Meaning. Emotion (Washington, D.C.). 12. 102-19. 10.1037/a0025167.

Lasaleta, J.D., Sedikides, Constantine and Vohs, K.D. (2014) Nostalgia weakens the desire for money. Journal of Consumer Research, 41, 713-729.

Zhou, X & Wildschut, Tim & Sedikides, Constantine & Shi, K & Feng, C. (2012). Nostalgia: the gift that keeps on giving. Journal of Consumer Research. 39.

Saad, Lydia (2008). JFK and Ronald Reagan Win Gallup Presidents Day Poll.

Batcho, Krystine. (1995). Nostalgia: A Psychological Perspective. Perceptual and motor skills. 80. 131-43. 10.2466/pms.1995.80.1.131.

Eklliot, Stuart (2009). In Trying Times, Nostalgia Returns.

Repa, Barbara (2013). Elder Abuse: Financial Scams against Seniors.

6. Lucky Loyalty Effect

Walker Reczek, Rebecca & L. Haws, Kelly & Summers, Christopher. (2014). Lucky Loyalty: The Effect of Consumer Effort on Predictions of Randomly Determined Marketing Outcomes. Journal of Consumer Research. 41. 1065-1078. 10.1086/678052.

Kivetz, Ran & Simonson, Itamar. (2003). The Idiosyncratic Fit Heuristic: Effort Advantage as a Determinant of Consumer Response to Loyalty Programs. Journal of Marketing Research - J MARKET RES-CHICAGO. 40. 454-467. 10.1509/jmkr.40.4.454.19383.

7. Sunk Cost Fallacy

Arkes, Hal & Blumer, Catherine. (1985). The psychology of sunk cost. Organizational Behavior and Human Decision Processes. 35. 124-140. 10.1016/0749-5978(85)90049-4.

Ho, Teck & Png, Ipl & Reza, Sadat. (2013). Sunk Cost Fallacy in Driving the World's Costliest Cars. SSRN Electronic Journal. . 10.2139/ssrn.2254483.

Shampanier, Kristina & Mazar, Nina & Ariely, Dan. (2007). Zero as a Special Price: The True Value of Free Products. Marketing Science. 26. 742-757. 10.1287/mksc.1060.0254.

8. Endowment Effect

Knetsch & Sinden, J.A.. (1984). Willingness to Pay and Compensation Demanded: Experimental Evidence of an Unexpected Disparity in Measures of Value. The Quarterly Journal of Economics. 99. 507-521.

Kahneman, Daniel & Knetsch, Jack & Thaler, Richard. (1991). The Endowment Effect, Loss Aversion, and Status Quo Bias. Journal of Economic Perspectives. 5. 193-206. 10.1257/jep.5.1.193.

Carmon, Ziv & Ariely, Dan. (2000). Focusing On The Forgone: How Value Can Appear So Different To Buyers And Sellers, "Journal. Journal of Consumer Research. 27. 360-70. 10.1086/317590.

Hossain, Tanjim & List, John. (2009). The Behavioralist Visits the Factory: Increasing Productivity Using Simple Framing Manipulations. National Bureau of Economic Research, Inc, NBER Working Papers. 58. . 10.2307/23359584.

9. IKEA Effect

I. Norton, Michael & Mochon, Daniel & Ariely, Dan. (2012). The IKEA effect: When labor leads to love. Journal of Consumer Psychology. 22. 453–460. 10.1016/j.jcps.2011.08.002.

Franke, Nikolaus & Piller, Frank. (2004). Value Creation by Toolkits for User Innovation and Design: The Case of the Watch Market. Journal of Product Innovation Management. 21. 401 - 415. 10.1111/j.0737-6782.2004.00094.x.

10. Confirmation Bias

C Wason, Peter. (1960). On the Failure to Eliminate Hypotheses in a Conceptual task. Quarterly Journal of Experimental Psychology - QUART J EXP PSYCHOL. 12. 129-140. 10.1080/17470216008416717.

Snyder, Mark. (1979). Testing Hypotheses about Other People: The Use of Historical Knowledge. Journal of Experimental Social Psychology - J EXP SOC PSYCHOL. 15. 330-342. 10.1016/0022-1031(79)90042-8.

Knobloch-Westerwick, Silvia & Meng, Jingbo. (2009). Looking the Other Way Selective Exposure to Attitude-Consistent and Counterattitudinal Political Information. Communication Research - COMMUN RES. 36. 426-448. 10.1177/0093650209333030.

Lamarre, Heather & Landreville, Kristen & Beam, Michael. (2009). The Irony of Satire. International Journal of Press-politics - INT J PRESS-POLIT. 14. 212-231. 10.1177/1940161208330904.

M. Kahan, Dan. (2013). Ideology, Motivated Reasoning, and Cognitive Reflection. Judgment and Decision Making. 8. 407-424.

11. Present Bias

UK Office for National Statistics (2016). Occupational Pension Schemes Survey: Self-Command in Practice, in Policy, and in a Theory of Rational Choice.

B. Detweiler, Jerusha & T. Bedell, Brian & Salovey, Peter & Pronin, Emily & J. Rothman, Alexander. (1999).

Message Framing and Sunscreen Use: Gain-Framed Messages Motivate Beach-Goers. Health psychology : official journal of the Division of Health Psychology, American Psychological Association. 18. 189-96. 10.1037/0278-6133.18.2.189.

Tversky, Amos & Kahneman, Daniel. (1981). The Framing of Decisions and The Psychology of Choice. Science (New York, N.Y.). 211. 453-8. 10.1126/science.7455683.

C. Schelling, Thomas. (1984). Self-Command in Practice, in Policy, and in a Theory of Rational Choice. American Economic Review. 74. 1-11.

Milkman, Katherine & Leonard Beshears, John. (2008). Mental accounting and small windfalls: Evidence from an online grocer. Journal of Economic Behavior & Organization. 71. 384-394. 10.1016/j.jebo.2009.04.007.

Ariely, Dan & Wertenbroch, Klaus. (2002). Procrastination, Deadlines, and Performance: Self-Control by Precommitment. Psychological science. 13. 219-24. 10.1111/1467-9280.00441.

12. Optimism Bias

D. Weinstein, Neil. (1980). Unrealistic Optimism About Future Life Events. Journal of Personality and Social Psychology. 39. 806-820. 10.1037/0022-3514.39.5.806.

Price, Paul & C Pentecost, Heather & D Voth, Rochelle. (2002). Perceived Event Frequency and the Optimistic Bias: Evidence for a Two-Process Model of Personal Risk

Judgments. Journal of Experimental Social Psychology. 38. 242-252. 10.1006/jesp.2001.1509.

Sharot, Tali. (2011). The optimism bias. Current biology : CB. 21. R941-5. 10.1016/j.cub.2011.10.030.

Cho, Hichang & Lee, Jae-Shin & Chung, Siyoung. (2010). Optimistic bias about online privacy risks: Testing the moderating effects of perceived controllability and prior experience. Computers in Human Behavior. 26. 987-995. 10.1016/j.chb.2010.02.012.

Jolls, Christine & Sunstein, C. (2006). The Law of Implicit Bias. Harvard Law School John M. Olin Center for Law, Economics and Business Discussion Paper Series. 94. . 10.2307/20439057.

13. Hedonic Adaptation

D Nelson, Leif & Meyvis, Tom. (2008). Interrupted Consumption: Disrupting Adaptation to Hedonic Experiences. Journal of Marketing Research - J MARKET RES-CHICAGO. 45. 654-664. 10.1509/jmkr.45.6.654.

D. Nelson, Leif & Meyvis, Tom & Galak, Jeff. (2009). Enhancing the Television-Viewing Experience through Commercial Interruptions. Journal of Consumer Research. 36. 160-160. 10.1086/597030.

Tella, Adedeji. (2007). The Impact of Motivation on Student's Academic Achievement and Learning Outcomes in Mathematics among Secondary School Students in Nigeria. Eurasia Journal of Mathematics, Science & Technology Education. 3. 10.12973/ejmste/75390.

Quoidbach, Jordi & Dunn, Elizabeth. (2013). Give It Up A Strategy for Combating Hedonic Adaptation. Social Psychological and Personality Science. 4. 563-568. 10.1177/1948550612473489.

14. Negativity Bias

Czapiński, J. (1985). Negativity bias in psychology: An analysis of Polish publications. Polish Psychological Bulletin, 16(1), 27-44.

Baumeister, Roy & Bratslavsky, Ellen & Finkenauer, Catrin & de Vohs, K. (2001). Bad Is Stronger than Good. Review of General Psychology. 5. 10.1037/1089-2680.5.4.323.

Brickman, Philip & Coates, Dan & Janoff-Bulman, Ronnie. (1978). Lottery Winners and Accident Victims: Is Happiness Relative?. Journal of personality and social psychology. 36. 917-27. 10.1037/0022-3514.36.8.917.

Lalwani, Ashok. (2006). Negativity and positivity biases in product evaluations: The impact of consumer goals and prior attitudes.

Nguyen, Viet Hoang & Claus, Edda. (2013). Good news, bad news, consumer sentiment and consumption behavior. Journal of Economic Psychology. 39. 426–438. 10.1016/j.joep.2013.10.001.

15. Bottom Dollar Effect

Soster, Robin & D. Gershoff, Andrew & Bearden, William. (2014). The Bottom Dollar Effect: The Influence of

Spending to Zero on Pain of Payment and Satisfaction. Journal of Consumer Research. 41. 656-677. 10.1086/677223.

A. Kahneman, Daniel & N. Tversky, Amos. (1979). Prospect Theory: An Analysis of Decision Under Risk. Econometrica. 47. 263-91. 10.2307/1914185.

Thaler, Richard. (1980). Toward a Positive Theory of Consumer Choice. Journal of Economic Behavior & Organization. 1. 39-60. 10.1016/0167-2681(80)90051-7.

Bagchi, Rajesh & Block, Lauren. (2011). Chocolate Cake Please! Why Do Consumers Indulge More When It Feels More Expensive?. Journal of Public Policy & Marketing. 30. 10.2307/23209282.

Loewenstein, George & Prelec, Drazen. (1998). The Red and the Black: Mental Accounting of Savings and Debt. Marketing Science. 17. 4-28. 10.1287/mksc.17.1.4.

Thaler, Richard. (1985). Mental Accounting and Consumer Choice. Marketing Science. 4. 199-214. 10.1287/mksc.4.3.199.

One Final Gem

Have you seen the Product Gems Behavioural Science Card Deck?

The card deck is a collection of 40 flashcards that each distil a piece of behavioural science research into easy-to-understand *gems* suggesting ways to apply the findings to the design of your products.

Visit

PRODUCTGEMS.IO

to find out more about the card deck, all the other books in the Product Gems series, and much, much more.

Printed in Great Britain
by Amazon